TRAIL
OF
THOUGHTS

BY

DAVID L. LOMAX

Published in the United States of America by Lomax Family, LLC.

ISBN:

979-8-9988263-3-7 (Paperback)
979-8-9988263-4-4 (Hardcover)
979-8-9988263-2-0 (E-Book)
979-8-9988263-5-1 (AudioBook)

MAP OF ALASKA

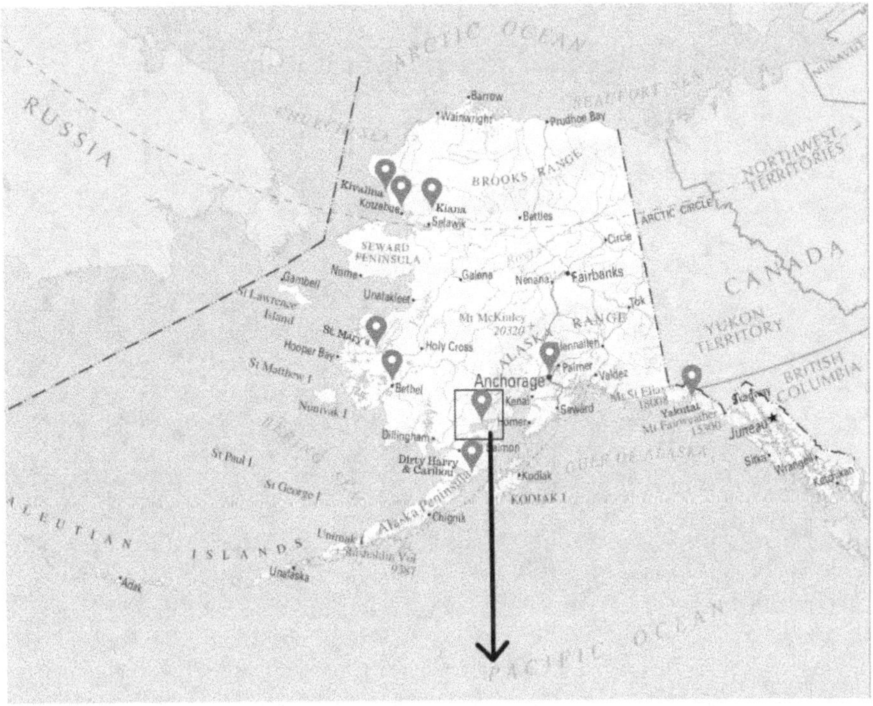

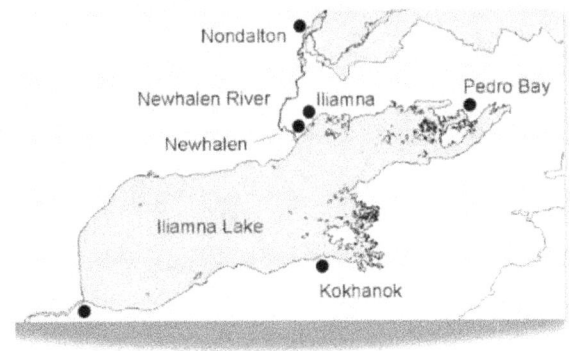

DEDICATION AND ACKNOWLEDGEMENT

This book is dedicated to my beloved son, Robert. It was his gentle insistence and heartfelt hope that I share my trail of thoughts that gave me the courage to tell this story. His belief in me, even when I doubted myself, has been my greatest gift and motivation.

I would also like to acknowledge my dear wife, Marcela, whose unwavering love, support, and help in the production of this book made it possible.

CONTENTS

CHAPTER 1
Southbound

How many more miles would I drive before taking the truck out of four-wheel drive? It had to be soon.

I had just driven out of the extreme cold. I'd left Alaska, and as I headed into warmer weather in Canada, I noticed snowless patches of ground as I drove deeper south, mile after mile. The highway seemed strange; where it was visible, the road was the color of clay and very bumpy. The uneven road caused strong vibrations that radiated to the vehicle's cab and my entire body. I rolled down the window of the white 1995 Dodge truck and felt the cold air on my fingertips, which made me feel refreshed and alive. I felt a sense of freedom.

My heart was full of joy now because I was wearing a sweater rather than a thick winter coat. The winter nights had been so cold that I'd feared turning off the truck might freeze the radiator and do internal damage to the engine since it had no heater block. Cold-starting motors in subzero temperatures can do tremendous harm to engines. When I crossed the Canadian *border, it was so cold I slept in the truck and kept the engine running. Through-out the night, I checked the gauges. During the day, I took no chances; I drove gingerly to avoid adding stress to the truck's mechanical operation.*

As I traveled, I noticed the trees were fuller and bigger than those farther north. I have always loved big pine trees. They are magnificent, standing tall and looking down on the world. The long, broad branches overhung the ground, and the thick green needles bristled from them, adding depth and softness to these mammoths.

I was in awe of just how old some of these beautiful giants of the forest were. They have so much history. Some part of me wished they could talk. Imagine the lessons we could learn from these guardians of the forest. It was like a dream, and I felt at peace. It was January 6, 1998, the sun was rising in a cloudless sky, and I had recently turned thirty-three. It was a good day to be alive.

Something had been missing for quite some time, though. I had needed a break from work and business and the dark, frigid, snowy winter that Alaska is well-known for. Alaska winters are long, and I had started to get cabin fever. I needed a prescription to heal, and sunshine was what the doctor ordered. So, when my stepfather asked me to do him a favor and drive his truck to Mexico, where he spent the winter, I was more than willing to oblige. I had just gotten a new job with the Alaska Department of Housing and Urban Development (HUD). The job allowed me to stay in town most of the time, giving me the flexibility and opportunity to continue developing properties. I was extremely grateful that my new boss had given me time off to go on this trip.

The plan was to avoid scratching the truck, save as much money as possible by reducing trip expenses, and repay my stepfather for some funds he'd given me. It would be challenging because I had spent everything I had on my fledgling business, which meant, at times, sleeping in the truck in the cold.

Driving down the highway in Canada, I wondered why the road was so bumpy, especially because, like Alaskans, Canadians have great equipment to clear ice and snow off roads. I reduced my speed to forty-five miles per hour. I had been driving long enough and it was time to make a pit stop.

Pulling over would give me a chance to check out the road. As I applied the brakes, the truck started to slide. Strange, I don't see any ice.

Finally, the truck came to a complete stop. Making sure it was parked safely on the wide shoulder, I carefully looked around to see if anybody was coming. Nope, it seemed clear. It was still early in the morning, so there were very few vehicles on the road. As I opened the door and looked down at the road, I saw that the top surface had a thin layer of black ice covering it. It is called that because it is difficult to see the ice while driving. This creates extremely hazardous driving conditions, especially at night.

I stepped out of the truck and immediately slipped on the road. I began sliding around, almost out of control and had to grab onto the door handle to hold myself up. Damn, this is slick. Making my way around to the opposite side of the truck, which was parked on a slight incline, proved challenging. After a short while, I made it around and finally reached the edge of the shoulder.

The next day, I decided I could no longer sleep in the truck and intended to find a hotel or something with a parking garage so I could lie in a warm bed. Luckily, I found a bed-and-breakfast late in the evening. The elderly owners welcomed me with that warm Canadian hospitality they are known for. Not only did I have a warm room to sleep in, but the husband offered to park the truck inside their garage. He told me it was -31 degrees Celsius, the same as the night before, and too cold for the truck to stay outside. I was so grateful to them.

BORN IN THE BAY AREA in November of 1964, I was a California boy and liked it. Back then, it was paradise on earth. I mean, it wasn't the good old days; it was the "great" old days. We had excellent schools and good friends, Little League baseball, skateboarding, motorcycling, a backyard swimming pool my grandfather built, boating, water skiing, fishing, car races, live 49ers games at Candlestick Park, and from time to time, we flew to Baja, Mexico, to fish for yellowfin tuna and much more.

One of my favorite activities was flying in or out of San Francisco Airport in a private Piper Twin Comanche and catching sight of the Golden Gate Bridge either on the way there or back from our cabin. I loved the beautiful low-level fog blanketing the mountains and bay, gently wrapping around the bridge. It always made me feel relaxed and at peace, as if I were in another world. I never got enough of that view.

The family partnered with another family and rapidly grew into a large, flourishing residential developer, building higher-end condominiums. The partners were good friends, and we children attended the same schools. One day, the fathers of each family decided to expand their business by moving to Anchorage, Alaska, and they quickly made their mark, adding to the skyline.

Not knowing what to expect, we landed in Anchorage in the summer of 1975. My mind was still in California. Elton John had just released *Captain Fantastic* and *KISS* was gearing up for their big shows. I hoped they'd come to Alaska the following year for the bicentennial celebration. As the plane descended, I thought of my best friend Jimmy. We'd just seen the movies *Tommy* and *Jaws*. After seeing *Jaws*, we were too scared to go shark fishing with his dad in the bay. I missed him; we were like brothers. *God rest his soul.*

Alaska is known as the "Last Frontier" for good reason. With an area of approximately 663,300 square miles and over three million lakes, there is plenty of room for folks to explore. As the largest state in the union, it is one-fifth the size of the lower forty-eight states and two times larger than Texas. It is easy to recognize just how significant this great state is and how much freedom it offers, the freedom to explore the limitless frontier lands. Upon our arrival, the state had a small population of just over 400,000 people. One could fly around for days on end and never see another soul. At that time, there were still places where human beings had never walked. There might still be some areas like that today. The vastness of the land

and the independence it demands are what make Alaska so mysterious and alluring.

The land of the midnight sun is vastly different from California. Summers are short and have a mixture of cool to hot weather that can change within moments.

Green forest wilderness surrounded by large snow-capped mountain ranges, lakes, rivers, waterfalls, and abundant wildlife is breathtakingly beautiful. I'm referring specifically to Anchorage, the largest city in the state, with a population of approximately 174,000, and the third-largest city by land area in the USA, covering just over 1,900 square miles.

The Cook Inlet waters, named after Captain James Cook, who explored the area in 1778, surround most of Anchorage and are a semi-enclosed estuary with one of the highest tides in the world. The tidal height averages thirty feet. Seeing how far the tides extend out from the shore is something to see.

Coming from the temperate climate of California, I had to quickly adapt and learn how to work and play in Alaska's short summers and long, dark, freezing winters.

Winters are a little bit different from summers. They are harsh, long, dark, freezing cold, snowy, and stormy. Occasionally, particularly in Anchorage, a climate event occurs, a phenomenon known as "Chinook storms." High winds blow warm air that rapidly melts the snow and ice, leaving the ground wet and muddy and creating a mess on the roads. Then, once the storms recede, all that mud and water freeze back.

As with many people, winters would sometimes bring me down, but most of my complaints stemmed from working outside in pitch-black conditions during subzero temperatures. Add the wind chill factor, and everything felt much colder. No matter how much I complained, I did enjoy many winter sports activities.

I downhill and cross country skied, snowmobiled, and played hockey when I was younger. If it was a winter sport, more than likely, I participated in it. I was even on the junior high school cross-country ski race team that went to state and placed eighteenth. I will never forget that race because about fifty yards from the finish line, my glove slipped off my hand, taking my pole with it, so I had to finish the race with just one ski pole in hand. The announcer said, "Here comes another one without a pole." I just started laughing while crossing the finish line because I thought I was the only one who had lost a glove and a ski pole that day.

The one winter sport that I enjoyed the most was snow machining. Others call it snowmobiling, but I like the term snow machining. Whenever I could catch a ride with a friend, I would try not to turn them down. Of course, my favorite activities were in the summer months.

I loved driving boats on rivers and lakes, but my absolute favorite activity was flying floatplanes. It is difficult to describe the beauty of flying over the lush landscape and having the freedom to land and take off at any of the millions of lakes and rivers of our choice. Even flying around the Bay Area, there is still nothing in the world I can compare it to, due to the immense size and scenic beauty of Alaska. If you love the outdoors, Alaska is ground zero for outdoor activity.

CHAPTER 2
Big Picture

I wanted to enjoy my 4,000-mile trip. Man, I have to pee. I've been holding it in for a long time since the last stop. *After pulling over onto the shoulder and getting out to relieve myself, I looked up toward the sky and stared at the big, exquisite trees and mountains. I felt at peace. Canada is such a big and beautiful country. Canadian citizens were usually courteous, kind, and warm to me. The country and its people warmed me, almost as if I were home.* I had better start driving if I want to reach Washington state tonight, *I thought.*

I began to reflect on my life, which had been both blessed and cursed at the same time. I had seen and done much, and I had worked hard to improve myself since my days in the bush by operating two businesses, holding full-time employment, and attending night college. I was constantly trying to figure out why my life had been in jeopardy more times than I cared to remember.

Bumping along the icy highway, that question hounded me. Someone or something had saved me again and again, but what for? What could be the reason? I am a complicated guy with many flaws and faults. Heaven knows I have made plenty of mistakes and done many stupid things in my life. I have burned a few bridges, some I regret. Most I do not. I fight for what is right. I am not always right, but when I am convinced about something, I try to stand up for myself, even at great cost.

My thoughts returned to the road when I stepped on the accelerator and noticed the truck sliding around while in four-wheel drive. I would have to continue driving super slowly until I cleared the ice. What a pain in the ass, but this was not my truck.

It was getting close to dinnertime. I found a place to eat and wondered if they served salads and had a phone. It would be good to check in with a family member in Alaska to let them know I'm okay. Pulling into the driveway and looking at the little diner sign made my stomach growl even more loudly. I opened the truck door and got out, then slipped to my knees and struggled to get back on my feet. The ground was covered with ice, and I was lucky not to get injured. Outside the small restaurant, there was a pay phone I could use. I was glad the weather was not cold, so I called to check in.

"Is everything fine?" I was asked.

"So far, there are no problems," I replied. "I slept in the truck in the freezing cold, but the temperature is warming up quickly. The only real problem I'm having is avoiding semi-trucks. They pass me with their double trailers on sharp, icy corners. I've been dealing with that since I started my trip in Alaska. The Canadian customs officer I talked with at the border told me it's not their problem."

"You'll just have to avoid them. When do you think you'll cross into the States?" I was asked.

"I still have to drive slowly due to the icy conditions. I think it's only about an hour or two to the border of Washington. After crossing the border, I'll get a hotel room."

"Are you tired?"

"No, not at all," I said. *"I want to take a shower."*

"Drive slowly. Take care and call me when you get across the border." I hung up the phone. *Oh boy! I could not wait to have some salad.*

I decided to eat as fast as I could and get going ASAP. Once I got a good night's rest in Washington, I planned to get up early and try to make it to Oregon. Heading back to the truck after dinner, I slipped on the ice while making my way down the stairs. As I walked up to the truck and looked down the road, I wondered if Canadians still referred to this highway as "the Alaska Highway." I noticed the ice was still the same grayish clay color. This was common; it can be warm outside, but ice can still remain on the road. The temperature seemed to be around 30 or 32 degrees Fahrenheit.

Slow, I must drive very slowly, *I repeated to myself.*

The highway was still bumpy, and there seemed to be a lot of traffic, including more monstrous semi-trucks. Looking down at the speedometer, it showed thirty-five miles per hour.

This is ridiculous, driving so slow on a major highway, *I thought.* It will be a long time before I reach the border.

It seemed strange that I couldn't muster the nerve to drive faster, since I have always been a little hyper, maybe more than a little, but I felt safe driving at that speed.

As I looked up at the road without warning, the world went dark.

I COULD NOT have been happier to get time off from work in the freezing weather. As I traveled southbound on the Alaska Highway at the southern end of Canada, I was thinking about the two small, fledgling businesses I had created that were starting to pay dividends, both financially and emotionally.

My primary business was renovating and selling old houses that required extensive work. Self-determination and entrepreneurship gave me great reassurance that I could forge my path in this world. I had a lot of passion, but sometimes, you only really know for sure once you are put to the test. I was proud of myself for what I had accomplished, especially under the circumstances I was dealing with.

I stumbled upon my second business while remodeling one of my properties. When I discovered that it was zoned for residential and commercial property, I quickly capitalized on my good fortune and turned it, and the others, into daily rentals. The houses were located near the international airport and the world's largest seaplane base, where hunters, fishermen, and tourists charter floatplanes. The concept was simple: I would rent the entire house instead of just a room, and include free airport pickup.

I gave my customers a great place to stay. It was a home away from home, with all the amenities, including kitchen items, fax machines, video recorders, outdoor hot tubs, garages, barbecue grills, washers, dryers, maid service, and just about everything a person could need. I also included an outdoor sink for cleaning fish and large freezers for preserving their cash of the day. I even installed and putting greens in the backyards.

The properties were private, and customers loved their privacy. I also wanted the international clients to be comfortable, so I'd raise a flag from their country of origin. This way, they felt more welcome and at home. If they didn't feel like cooking, they could walk down the street to a legendary Alaska restaurant in just a few minutes. I couldn't ask for a better location.

Brochure for Graceland Cottages
Model, My Dog, Robert, & Self

Seaplane Base for Cottage Houses

Since the houses were commercially zoned, I had to pay a bed tax, but that zoning also legitimized and helped grow my business. For a college class, I wrote a business plan and was surprised to learn my instincts were right: the location and extra services gave me a competitive edge over nearby hotels.

People told me I was crazy for renting my houses to tourists.

"That's nuts!" they'd say, chuckling.

After I proved them wrong, some of them wanted to get in on the action.

For years, I noticed a strange pattern: the more I accomplished, whether attending night college, flipping houses, or hosting tourists, the more resentment I seemed to attract. The same people who I knew didn't care about me before grew even angrier as I found success. I never understood why. I've never resented anyone for doing well; if anything, I found their success motivating. It made me work harder, not bitter.

To me, money was just a tool, no different than a hammer or saw, useful only for building something meaningful. Business, like surfing, is all about timing and position. Even the best surfers miss waves, but they don't quit; they adjust and try again. Some call it luck, but I see it as an opportunity.

I've always respected those who fail and keep going. People who don't give up often become the biggest winners. I've made plenty of mistakes, some of them pretty dumb, but oddly, those failures became the foundation for my biggest successes.

But I'm not writing to discuss business. This isn't about money or strategy. It's about something more profound that happens inside when effort is met with judgment, when you're misunderstood, and while you're privately fighting the hardest physical and psychological battles no one else sees. Sometimes, the most experienced surfers can miss a wave for whatever reason.

One day, my flight instructor, who taught me to fly and bravely let me solo his plane when I was fifteen, pointed at an aviation map and told me, "Look at the big picture. Don't fixate on little events. We will get to the small details later. Don't worry about the little lakes or low-lying hills.

Look at the big mountains and lakes, they are easier to see from the air." Because he was a mentor and friend, I listened carefully and took nothing he told me for granted.

The man who raised me tried to teach me the same thing. "Don't sweat the small stuff," he'd say, but that went in one ear and out the other, and it never dawned on me what he meant until my flight instructor explained it. Although he did not articulate many lessons, I was fortunate and grateful to have observed him closely. At times, he told me that he was not a teacher. That was not true. I did gain an immense amount of knowledge from him. I don't think he had a clue that I paid close attention and absorbed his work ethic and lessons like a sponge.

The concept of simplifying complex reasoning provided me with another tool to approach certain situations more positively.

Applying lessons like these slowly chipped away barriers in my head, but imprinting them took some time. My biggest problem was the way I saw myself.

Being a shy, self-doubting young child made things somewhat challenging for me. I was my harshest critic. If I failed at something, I felt a deep sense of loss.

Being a perfectionist can create difficulty in many aspects of one's life and can play cruel tricks. I have always wanted to do something great, to create something fantastic for myself and others. In my youth, I often falsely believed I would never achieve much success, especially when I had to read or write school assignments. When my elementary teachers asked me to read aloud or turn in a written assignment, I would shake and break out in a cold sweat in front of my classmates. However, I understood oral assignments and successfully executed them. I did not know why I was having so much trouble with English. I was not aware of any learning alternatives that could help me.

It wasn't until my senior year that I learned I had dyslexia. A family member told me they had known that for years, I had that problem, but I have no memory of anyone talking to me about it. I never told them how I felt incredible frustration, shame, and humiliation concerning that problem. The great equalizer for me was that I had a combination of strong mechanical skillsets and athletic abilities that gave me some confidence around my friends, classmates, and, at times, my family.

Looking back, I think dealing with that type of learning disability was one of the reasons I became a perfectionist. I wanted to make up for my inadequacies. I wanted so badly to please my family, so whatever manual job I did, I worked excessively hard to perfect it, which proved futile. I have worked hard and taken great pride in my accomplishments, but I have also had many doubts. Trying to be a perfectionist seems silly to me now. For whom and what?

CHAPTER 3

Kiana

*P*ain. *I remember being in pain.*

God help me! *I shouted in my head.*

My eyes opened. What was going on? I was having a difficult time breathing.

What's that?

I felt a strange sensation in my left hand. As I rolled my eyes, I saw a man standing outside the 1995 white Dodge truck.

It seems cold. Why is it cold?

A strange man was petting my bloody left hand, and I could hear him say, "You're going to live."

"No, not if you don't get this steering wheel off of me," *I replied in a weak, withering voice, convinced that my thirty-three years of life were quickly coming to an end.*

"The police and ambulance are on their way. It should take around twenty minutes for them to arrive," he stated.

I thought help had already arrived. It's tough to breathe. Twenty minutes? There is no way I can last that long! I'm stuck.

My mind flashed back to memories of spending summers north of the Arctic Circle during my teenage years. Although those months were primarily defined by having to perform the work of a full-grown man well before my teen years and living in conditions that could, at best, be called spartan, I managed to have some fun, especially when my cousins came to visit. Those guys were cool. I loved being around them. We had so much fun. Sometimes, during the evening, we would all go to the dump and shoot at bottles. I loved hearing the crack of the rifle. In the distance, you could see a perfectly good bottle sitting there, then shatter it into a thousand pieces. Cool!

When duty called, we would fly to a remote location and hunt caribou and moose for my stepfather's work crews to eat. My cousin's father was a professional butcher, and he taught us how to debone the animals where they lay so that the meat would be lighter for us to carry to the airplane.

Mostly, I remember adventures related to the Native villages north of the Arctic Circle, connected by the 380-mile Kobuk River and adventures near and around Lake Iliamna, the largest lake in Alaska.

THE PARTNERSHIP QUICKLY DISSOLVED, and my stepfather took over the company independently. As a man of action, he bravely rolled the dice, taking a large risk to help improve Alaskan Natives' housing conditions. It wasn't long before he reached greater heights by becoming the largest Native housing contractor in the state.

There were many obstacles to overcome. The first one that comes to mind is workers' safety. Most villages at that time lacked adequate medical facilities. Communications were often down, and the weather was unpredictable, creating another hazard to contend with. Pilots, aircraft, and other modes of transportation may not be available even if the weather is good. So, what does one do when they are seriously hurt? Bleed to death or get gangrene while waiting for help. Another obstacle is logistics.

All building materials, including food, clothing, and toiletries, had to be brought in by air, barge, and boat. Many villages had no access to roads, phones, water, sewers, or walkways; helicopters delivered the material to the lot sites in those subdivisions without roads. Overcoming the complexities of logistics took an enormous amount of organization and transportation support to build the houses. That was the reality of working in the villages.

When I was fourteen, after school ended, I spent my first summer in Kiana, about fifty-seven air miles east of Kotzebue and around thirty miles north of the Arctic Circle. The name Kiana means "Place Where Three Rivers Meet." It sits on a bluff overlooking two rivers the Kobuk and Squirrel rivers. Currently, there are about 360 residents, most of whom are Iñupiat Eskimos.

During the summer, from late May to early October, average temperatures range from 40 to 60 degrees Fahrenheit, and rainfall averages around 16 inches per year. Of course, being north of the Arctic Circle, temperatures can be extreme, ranging from 90 to -54 degrees Fahrenheit. When the river freezes for the rest of the year, residents travel from village to village on snow machines. I even knew people who drove trucks on the frozen river. At -54 degrees Fahrenheit, not including the wind chill factor, I'd rather be inside a heated truck cab than outside on a snow machine.

I met Larry and his wife when I first arrived in Kiana. They had two children, Paula and Pat, who were about my age. Larry was a professional hunting and fishing guide. A short, stocky, half Iñupiat Eskimo who had grown up in Kiana, he was a man of many talents. He knew a lot of the old

Native customs and took pride in his people and heritage. Because he cared so much about his people, he selflessly became a state trooper to help them.

His father grew up on a farm in "the lower 48" on the West Coast and moved to Alaska to get away from cows. As a young man, he got a job as a gold prospector, which led him to live in Kiana. He shared many dangerous and exciting adventures from his life and told us he knew where much of the gold was in the area, but I don't think he told anyone where it was. They were a prominent family and even owned the only grocery store in the area. Larry's mother was an Iñupiat Eskimo, and his brother, Vic, was the mayor. Vic, who was always very nice to me, seemed fairly happy whenever I talked with him. He told us that he had trouble falling asleep and struggled to wake up. We lovingly called him the sleeping mayor. I liked the whole family.

Because of the significant difficulties of building in the Arctic, my stepfather's innovative designs, and the fact that he made local hiring a top priority, *National Geographic* took notice and wrote an article about the company and co-partner Vic.[1] During the summer of 1981, twenty-six units were built in Kiana and the surrounding villages of Noorvik, Selawik, Ambler, Shungnak, and Kobuk, totaling 170 units.

My stepfather hired a filmmaker and made short movies of the construction of his houses for HUD, which he would send back to Washington, D.C. "Show the insulation make sure you show how thick it is in the ceilings and floors," Larry would shout out as I helped the director carry his equipment around to locations. After my acting debut, I quickly learned just how tough Hollywood was. At fourteen, I was already a "has-been."

A few days before shooting the movie, Larry had asked me if I wanted to water ski. "You'll be the first white boy to ski on the Kobuk River." I did not care about that; my biggest concern was how cold the water was. Larry continued to persuade me, and I reluctantly said yes, only because I could feel the heat of the blazing sun burning my body. The temperature was in the low 80s. The sun was intense because the Earth's axis shifts the northern hemisphere toward the sun. One wouldn't think people get sunburned north of the Arctic Circle, but many do. I didn't care about that. I loved the fact that it was no longer cold.

I just wanted to go for it and have some fun. Before that day, I had tried dipping my toes into the river once or twice, but that was as far as I'd gotten. I know what people say about me when it comes to cold water: "He's a baby." What can I say? That's the way my body was built. Needless to say, the river doesn't get super warm even when winter has receded. Still, I was determined to do this.

While sitting in the blue jet boat, I remembered the good times from my youth, growing up in California. We'd spend many weekends in our tiny cabin. That's where I learned how to water ski between the ages of six and eight. At that time, we had a powerful waterskiing jet boat. Equipped with a massive, Big Block Ford 460 Dual 4-Barrel Carburetors engine. It was loud, fast, and we had a great time running it. I helped take good care of the boat by constantly washing and waxing it, and assisted with its mechanical maintenance.

I loved those days being out there on that lake. Especially, because the weather in California was fantastic most of the year and the water was warm as well. I remember fishing from the docks for bass, bluegill, and catfish, but mostly bluegill. I caught catfish with my uncle, usually late in the evening. Sometimes, we even went gigging for frogs. Frog legs taste like chicken. They're pretty good, but I wouldn't want to eat them all the time.

The blue jet boat that would pull me on the Kobuk River was a little different than the jet boats I'd seen in the past. This boat was more like a utility workhorse equipped for fishing and hunting, capable of handling treacherous waterways, and was surprisingly fast.

Larry knew the Kobuk very well. I knew I could trust him to keep me safe on the river, which was among the longest in the Northwest. It has massive widths up to 1,500 feet, and drains into the Chukchi Sea. The river is teeming with sheefish, whitefish, salmon, and the great northern pike. While driving on the river, one must be careful when navigating a boat to avoid accidentally running aground on one of the many submerged sandbars. Exposed sandbars were scattered throughout the river, giving it a majestic appearance, especially when the river flows past vertical cliffs.

My primary concern was how to jump into the cold river without acting like a baby in front of everyone. *Oh man, this is going to be freaking cold.* Larry was laughing. "Get in the water. It's not cold," he said.

"Don't worry about the fish. Pikes only bite if you stand still."

What the hell is he talking about? Of course, it's not cold for him. He's accustomed to being in temperatures as low as -50 degrees Fahrenheit. Cold or not, now I had to worry about being bitten by a pike. *What the heck? I don't think he's joking because of what had happened to Larry's daughter Paula a few days before.* I had been fishing for whitefish within eyesight and earshot of Paula and her friends, who were laughing and swimming in the Kobuk. Suddenly, I heard Paula scream out, "A fish bit me, PIKE, PIKE!" I watched the kids screaming as they swam back to shore while she was still in the river, screaming, "PIKE!" She waded back to shore and when she got out of the water, I could see blood dripping down her lower leg. *I thought pikes only attacked near the shore, not in the middle of the river.*

The great northern pike's body is oddly shaped. Sure, it has fins and gills like other fish, but its facial features look more like a duck bill. According to Alaska Fish and Game, the upper jaws, roof of the mouth, and tongue are armed with hundreds of short razor teeth slanted backward, and the lower jaw has longer teeth to keep their prey from escaping. Their bodies have evolved with a streamlined, single-rayed dorsal fin that sits far back, allowing them to achieve quick bursts of speed to ambush their prey. Twenty pounds is about the average size, but they can grow up to thirty-eight pounds and reach a length of over four feet.[2] They are freshwater killing machines, similar to sharks.

I was familiar with pikes found in rivers and lakes because when I was a little younger, I caught small ones in lakes near Anchorage and I'd had to be careful of their sharp teeth. However, these were just small, twelve to sixteen-inch pikes, nothing really to harm anyone, although they can make your fingers bleed while removing hooks from their mouths. At an early age, I learned to use pliers to remove hooks from their mouths and to pick them up by the tail, then throw them back into the water. I had heard the stories of large northern pikes, but I'd never seen the likes of those before. Larry told me they have been known to attack ducks in the water. I guess they must be stealthy to sneak up on a duck. That's one mean fish.

Oh great! I thought. *Hmm, the first white boy to water ski in the Kobuk who cares? I had bigger things to think about, like getting into the water.*

Somehow, I got the courage to dive into the water. Lucky for me, I landed in a warmer pool of water. I didn't want to feel the cold pools I knew were out there. I just wanted to get up on the skis and have the sun warm me up.

"Are you ready?" the spotter, George, shouted.

Spotters assist the skiers, inform the drivers of the skiers' needs, and advise on whether to speed up or slow down, while also looking out for other boats. George was a young Iñupiat Eskimo and a very nice guy. Larry slowly drove the boat around as George tossed me the rope.

"Come on, David, you can do it!" shouted Larry. "Ready?"

I could hear the motor purring. My body was completely submerged in the water, and I pointed toward the boat approximately thirty feet in front of me. The ski tips were out of the water and moving ever so slowly. I hadn't stood up on a pair of skis since we left California. *I hope I can do this.* I started shaking from the cold water. I just wanted to get up.

"Yes," I shouted, giving him the thumbs-up signal.

The engine roared to life. I could feel the rope tug and water rushing all around me. I had to keep my tips straight and not allow my skis to wander around. If I couldn't resist the water pressure from the skis, my feet would twist outward, spreading my legs like doing the splits, which would make me fall, and I did not want that to happen. I could feel the pressure on my legs and hands as the boat pulled me through the water. Suddenly, I was going very fast. *I'm up, I made it! I'm actually standing upright water skiing! Thank God I did not fall back into the water.*

What a feeling of exhilaration! The warm air blowing through my hair and wrapping around me covered me like a warm blanket. I could hardly believe it. Here I was, water skiing in the great Kobuk River north of the Arctic Circle on a toasty, sunny day. Looking behind me, I could see the village of Kiana up on the hill. What a view! It seemed unreal, as if I were in a different world.

The roar of the outboard motor sent a chill up my spine. It was as though I was having a spiritual experience. I moved from side to side, trying to jump the boat's wake while continually looking for logs and other debris. Hitting something would have sucked.

Larry drove me near cliffs overlooking the river and large sandbars, which gave me the sensation of driving at one hundred miles an hour, even though we were probably only going twenty or thirty miles an hour. After a while, I saw George waving his hand, indicating it was time to let go of the rope. *Oh, man, not now.* I had just gotten warm and was enjoying myself. I did not want to let go and sink into the cold river. Suddenly, a memory from a few years earlier flashed in my head. While water skiing in the warm waters of Clearlake, California, where our cabin was located, a man who towed me behind his V-drive speedboat pulled me too close to a dock and wham! I hit it straight on. I was knocked out and I remember bobbing around in the water, hearing and seeing people screaming and jumping in after me. They pulled me up on the dock and drove me to the hospital, which was quite far away. I sustained a broken arm. Eventually, the arm healed, and I never had much problem with my left arm, even after my uncle came up with a bright idea to remove my cast with a hacksaw and pliers. I watched intensely as he kept sawing away, as we both laughed our behinds off. That night, we went fishing for catfish until five in the morning.

At least there weren't any docks around here to hit just some sandbars and boats that were parked on shore. No way was I going to hit anything this time. Even if I hit a sandbar, I did not believe I would get hurt, but I didn't want to look stupid. Then I would have to swim back to shore in that cold river, fighting currents, and there was no way I would do that. That would not be too smart. I just had to be a little careful because there were clusters of little fishing boats parked up and down the river, and I didn't want to hit any of them either.

Lesson learned from my earlier accident: Letting go of the rope was not going to be a problem. It is just a matter of where and when. I let go of the rope far enough from shore and away from the little fishing boats. Down I went into the cold river. Larry circled his boat around. I could see him laughing.

"You did it! You did it!"

Yeah, I did it, the first white kid. I just wanted to get out of the river fast. The first two feet of the water were somewhat warm. Below my waist and down to my feet, the water was freezing cold. *As guys would say, there was shrinkage.* The cold water reminded me of past days spent swimming in the icy waters of Lake Tahoe. I can tell you that I didn't swim long in that lake, because I was a chicken.

I quickly made my way to shore, thankful it was warm outside. While drying myself off, I could hear children swimming and having a good time in the distance. Why not? The summers north of the Arctic Circle are short. People should have fun before the temperatures get below zero. I was glad I did not live there in the winter; Anchorage was cold enough.

After wiping the water and sand off, it was time for a late afternoon snack. Walking up the steep road from the Kobuk River to the cooking area was no easy task. It took a lot of energy out of me to climb that hill. When I reached the top, I saw the first of many houses being built. As I walked by the first house, my mind quickly turned to my stomach.

I wonder if Rhoda made chocolate chip cookies? I thought. My stepdad had hired her to cook for the crew. A short, heavyset Iñupiat Eskimo who was warm and friendly and seemed to smile and laugh every time I saw her, she was an excellent cook. She'd laugh and tell me that one day she was going to make fish head stew for dinner. She'd say how the cheeks and eyes were her favorite. Finally, one night before dinner, I took a sneak peek inside a large steaming pot on the stove and saw fish heads bobbing up and down in the boiling water. Well, let's say that I did not eat that night. Instead, I filled myself with her mouthwatering cookies and a Snickers bar that reminded me of home. Rhoda always saved me some of her cookies, which she hid from the rest of the crew. I was the only one who knew the location. Her secret was safe with me.

Later that night, I learned that the Natives had tremendous respect for the wildlife they ate and did not waste any part of an animal's body. There is a deep-rooted respect for wildlife that sustains them and is embedded in their culture. Many in our non-Native cultures have learned bad habits and we are known as a "throwaway society." I found their culture and beliefs about being in harmony with nature to be beautiful and fascinating. What could be more loving than that?

While lying in bed that night, I wondered what the next day had to offer. Little did I know what was in store for me.

CHAPTER 4
Construction Techniques

To continue the story, flip to Chapter 5 unless you're interested in a description of building techniques in the Arctic.

CONSTRUCTION IN LARGER CITIES is complicated, even in the best of circumstances. However, working in the villages is beyond tough. Expenses can exponentially increase if supplies, materials, and tool replacements are miscounted, the further away from the larger towns, the higher the costs and greater the risk.

My stepfather's designs proved to be effective at a relatively low cost, especially in the northern part of the Arctic Circle. He had designed an adjustable foundation, setting the houses about three to four feet above the ground. The base of the foundations was made from four-by-four-foot wood pads placed on top of the Arctic tundra.

The tundra is a biome characterized by low temperatures and short growing seasons, which hinder tree growth. It acts like an insulation blanket covering the subsoil and keeping it permanently frozen during the blazing hot summers. Frozen soil is also known as permafrost. That is why great care had to be taken not to disturb the fragile tundra while installing the foundation pads, even though the top surface of the tundra had to be scraped off to lay down and level the pad.

The two, three, and four-bedroom homes were designed to function well in the Arctic. Each house usually had six to eight pads, depending on its size. A vertical, two-inch pipe mounted in the center of the pad supported the foundation. Then, a shorter metal sleeve slid over the threaded pipe, allowing the floors to be adjusted. Pipe sizes ranged from sixteen to twenty-four inches, depending on the terrain.

The foundation corner ends were fitted with adjustable steel lateral bracing attached to the base and fastened to the bottom of the foundation beams. The genius design of that system was that if the permafrost melted underneath the pads and the house shifted up or down, the homeowner could level their house with a pipe wrench.

The homes were purposely built high enough above ground so the permafrost beneath the foundation pads would not melt on hot summer days. Just the floor systems alone had R-36 insulation.

The houses also cantilevered over the foundation pads to ensure that the pads would be shaded and that the weight of the house would compress the permafrost, which helped keep the soil frozen.

While better and more effective foundations exist, this adjustable foundation was the ticket to keeping costs down.

High quality craftsmanship and innovative ideas implemented into the homes became my stepfather's trademark. Insulation and vapor barriers throughout the homes were critical. Triple-pane windows were installed and well-suited for the north's extreme conditions. He used R-49 insulation in the ceilings, about fifteen and a half inches thick. Weight and wood quality were critical, so he used kiln-dried two-by-six and two-by-four studs placed twenty-four inches on center throughout the exterior and interior walls. The cost of the kiln-dried lumber materials was significantly higher. Still, due to the reduced moisture content, he was able to save hundreds of thousands of dollars in transportation fuel costs associated with airplanes and helicopters.

He put the studs twenty-four inches on center for two main reasons. Again, transportation costs and reducing the outside cold air infiltration through each of the wood members. The California corner technique was utilized to enhance the insulation properties of the corners. R-19 insulation was carefully installed into each open cell.

The insulation installer had to ensure that no gaps were left open. This, in turn, added significant insulation properties to the house, thereby saving the homeowner thousands of dollars on their heating bill.

Vapor barriers were applied to all exterior walls, ceiling joists, and flooring within the house. They were crucial in preventing air infiltration. A vapor barrier is a plastic material that comes in long rolls and is stapled to the exterior stud walls and ceiling joists. The vapor barrier had to be sealed; overlaps and holes were taped to ensure the exterior walls and ceiling were airtight.

Now, the only area of the house vulnerable to air infiltration was the floor, which had to be sealed up. Somehow, he figured out vinyl was the solution. Known as "resilient flooring," the industry refers to it as such; it is strong and seals the floor, much like the vapor barrier on exterior walls and ceilings. He ensured the vinyl was laid before any interior walls were built to minimize the number of cuts in the vinyl and prevent it from curling up around the edges.

Vinyl came in long rolls and was so heavy that when one of the workers was helping to carry a roll, he dislocated his shoulder. Once the vinyl was glued, the interior walls were carefully built and installed to avoid scratching the resilient flooring. One could say these were green homes, but the term 'green construction' was not yet in use in those days. These houses were so airtight that they required an air exchange from the outside; otherwise, the people in the homes would run the risk of suffocation and/or bacterial growth. This system proved highly efficient in building house productivity.

There were several reasons that R-49 insulation was installed in the ceilings. One: The thicker insulation would help reduce heating expenses.

Two: The insulation kept icicles from forming on the roof's edges by keeping heat inside the house from rising through the ceiling and melting the snow on the roof, which would otherwise create icing. Over time, the constant heating and freezing can cause significant wear and tear on the roof.

The sun can cause snow to melt, and icicles can form. To counter the sun's energy, adequate ventilation was installed throughout the roof system. The ventilation system needed to be installed correctly because the attic and roof were required to remain frozen throughout the winter.

The ceiling joists were problematic due to the extreme temperatures from both outside and inside the home, so another innovative solution was needed. The problem was the massive expansion and contraction of the ceiling joist. When the outside temperature reaches a bone-chilling -54 degrees Fahrenheit, and the home's interior is at a comfortable 70 degrees Fahrenheit, the ceiling joists would expand. The ceiling would expand as much as one and a half inches or more at times. The solution was to install a panel ceiling before the vinyl flooring was laid down. After the installation was completed, then they painted the panel ceiling without worrying about overspray on the interior walls, as the interior wall paneling had not been installed at that time.

Soon after the ceiling was painted, the crews would put paneling on the exterior walls. He used paneling for two reasons: one, it was strong and durable and could withstand a lot of abuse, and two, it didn't need to be painted, which eliminated the cost of painting.

Fastening the wall to the floor was just a matter of nailing 16-penny nails through the bottom plate and into the subfloor. However, fastening the upper part of the ceiling was a little different. Due to the extreme expansion and contraction of the ceiling, special deflection clips had to be applied to the walls and fastened to the ceiling, allowing the ceiling to float independently of the walls. Paneling was then applied to the stud walls, and then the upper part of the trim was nailed onto the ceiling, not the walls, allowing it to float. Otherwise, if it were nailed to the wall, the trim would break apart to move in sync with the ceiling.

Another fascinating innovation he devised was the interior plumbing. Back then, many villages did not have indoor plumbing, a luxury most of us take for granted today. The plan was simple but highly effective and efficient. He designed a special interior wall system that supported a sanitary drainage plumbing tree made of copper piping, which sat on top of the floor and ran parallel to the kitchen, bathrooms, and oil boiler system. Since all the plumbing was inside the house, repairs could easily be made without going outside. The plumber could build the tree anywhere and slide it between the wall system for final assembly.

Oil was the primary commodity used by villagers to heat their houses. Still, they wanted homeowners to have an alternative heating source in case the boiler broke down, oil was unavailable for delivery, or there was a shortage of resources. He installed a wood-burning stove in the living room to ensure people did not freeze during the harsh winters. He was very safety-conscious, and I guess he may have learned that from aviation.

The oil-burning boiler furnace provided the central heating system and hot water source. A mixture of water and glycol, or antifreeze, went through the pipes, providing the home with constant, even heat. I never asked him why he didn't use forced air heat; he must have had a good reason, because the cost of copper pipe, materials, and transportation was expensive. Perhaps he believed it was the most effective heating system, or he had to comply with HUD regulations.

Instead of using standard plywood, tar paper, and asphalt shingles, steel roofing was incorporated into the homes. Because steel roofs were durable and strong, they could prevent leaks from rain, snow, and ice, and therefore didn't require plywood or tar paper. Instead, lightweight two-by-four purlins were used to reduce transportation costs and provide the carpenters with a safety benefit. Once the purlins were attached to the roof trusses, the crews could walk up and down them like a stepladder without worrying about falling.

However, snow and ice still posed a problem because walking on steel panels while it's snowing can be fatal. One slip and it's over.

The good news for carpenters is that they could still apply each sheet individually while standing on the purlins and completely screw it off without worrying too much about falling. Even when the roof had been laid down and secured, there were still other items to install, such as the ridge, gable caps, and other accessories, which could be problematic if there was snow and ice. Hence, carpenters had to be extra careful and figure out how to avoid falling.

The good news for homeowners is that steel roofs shed snow effectively. He did not want them to risk their lives by climbing on roofs and fighting the brutal elements to remove snow. Ideas like these may seem simple, but at the time, they were bold new ideas that helped promote the green construction revolution, or, more accurately, energy-efficient housing.

The construction of the homes became similar to an assembly line in a factory. By the end of the project, he was producing two houses a day, an impressive feat, given the location, north of the Arctic Circle. The homes were designed to withstand extreme temperatures, handle heavy snow and strong wind loads, and require minimal energy and maintenance, helping owners save significantly on operating costs. Funny enough, homeowners didn't complain about the quality; instead, they said the homes were too warm. They had to open windows in the middle of winter just to cool off.

Now that's a review! I wonder how many stars he'd get on Yelp today. I know I'd give him five.

Readers interested in learning more can refer to my PowerPoint presentation, "SJCC Construction Tech VDC," which is referenced in the notes at the back of this book.[3]

CHAPTER 5

Clear Air Turbulence

"Y ou are going to make it," said a police officer.

"No, you have to get that steering wheel off of me. I cannot breathe. I have a woofer somewhere. I need it," I said in a weak voice.

From time to time, I would have an allergic reaction that would trigger mild asthma, so that's why I referred to the woofer. Not fully comprehending the gravity of my situation, I thought I was having an allergic reaction.

I could only see the night sky on the right side with my peripheral vision. Lights flashed from the road, but nobody was trying to get me out.

Cold, I am so cold. Dad! Dad! I thought, calling out to my biological dad, Gordon, who had passed away when I was young. I'm freezing.

I could not turn my head, I could only move my eyes. Looking around, I could see the truck's cab crushed all around me. I wondered if I could move my feet. I hope I'm not paralyzed. I wiggled my toes a couple of times. Oh, yes, thank God, yes! I don't think I'm paralyzed, not yet, anyway.

As I wiggled my feet, I could hear the officer behind me thrashing around. What was he trying to do? He had not said another word. I could feel his hands on my back. Something was moving around. I felt pressure on my back and heard ripping noises along with his heavy breathing as he kept tugging and pulling.

What is he doing? He is not cutting me out.

"Can you breathe better now?" he asked.

Wheezing and taking shallow breaths, I remained silent as I concentrated on breathing. I soon realized that he was cutting the foam out of the seat back to relieve the pressure of the steering wheel crushing my lungs. I could feel him reaching down deeper and deeper, pulling out the foam in the seat to give me a little bit more room.

"Can you breathe?" the officer asked again.

I thanked him for getting a smidgen of the pressure off me, but noted that it wasn't enough. I don't know if he heard me.

My left hand was dangling outside the front window, and I could see blood dripping from it. I wondered if I had died and woken up. I knew I was still alive, but when I was out, I hadn't seen anything: no white light, no darkness, nothing. It was a complete blank. Maybe I had died, talked with somebody, and they put me back down here.

I knew I was seriously injured, but didn't know how badly. I have to get out of this truck, *I kept thinking. I was still gasping for air. I could only inhale less than half of my lung capacity, if that. It felt like I was suffocating. I tried to breathe deeper, but the intense pressure from the steering wheel wouldn't allow that. Each breath I took was like drinking little sips of water, which required intense focus. My eyes and toes were the only body parts I could move, so I continued to wiggle my toes while rolling my eyes around to assess my situation. I could see twisted metal all around me.*

No way out. Oh man, don't let me die in this place, not here, especially in the middle of nowhere. I did not want to die at all. I still had goals to fulfill, like getting married and having a family.

For some reason, I remained eerily calm. Somehow, I knew that panicking would have been disastrous for me and the people trying to help me. I was more concerned about people who were trying to help me. I did not want to put additional stress on them by constantly crying out that I was in pain. Besides, I could not feel that much pain or tell where the pain was located other than in my chest. Even my bloody left hand, which was still dangling out the driver's-side window of the truck, did not hurt. Still, I knew I was severely injured; I mean, really bad.

I probably should have been scared, but I wasn't. I just concentrated on controlling each breath, my only hope of survival. I didn't panic, maybe due to shock or perhaps because I was pinned in like a sardine and couldn't move. Or maybe it was because I was without a coat and freezing from the temperatures in the high 20s. I just don't know.

I think I am out of luck. My days are numbered. Dad, help me! *I kept thinking as I started to drift away again.*

MY LIFE HAS BEEN, at times, extremely challenging, and it hasn't turned out the way I expected. For starters, I didn't realize that I would spend most of my summers working in the bush starting around age fourteen, but that's how it turned out. The experiences there were unforgettable. I still contend with the harsh ones that seared my soul. Others, however, filled me with wonder.

I had seen the Northern Lights/ Aurora Borealis many times in and around Anchorage, but I was blown away when I saw them in Kiana. The colors were so bright and brilliant: green, blue, red, and yellow. I watched as they danced low along the midnight sky. It felt like I could reach out and touch them, though they are around sixty miles high in the atmosphere. *God, they are beautiful.*

The next morning, I told Rhoda, the camp cook, about what I had seen and how beautiful the sky looked during breakfast. She stared at me with a startled look in her eyes, then told me that the Native people go missing when the northern lights glow.

"When people see them by themselves, the lights take them away, and many Natives have disappeared," she said. "Don't go outside by yourself when they come out." I could tell she was genuinely scared for me, so I did not mention that I had stood alone watching them for twenty minutes the night before.

Over the years, my adopted state would provide similarly moving experiences. My grandfather would say to us all the time, "Alaska is a grand and beautiful place. A land so vast and untouched by people. If you don't like the weather, wait five minutes. A land of wonder. A land without mercy." I have never forgotten those words. Grandpa was a great and wise man who served in World War II. He loved reciting long verses from memory, especially the poem "The Cremation of Sam McGee" by Robert W. Service, which he wrote in 1907. Strangely enough, that is where I went to high school, named after him: Robert Service High. My grandfather was an avid reader, craftsman, and outdoorsman. Truly, he was a Renaissance man. To me, he was the best. I adored him. I was glad to have been around when I was a young child. *God rest his soul.*

Before I turned four, my biological parents moved frequently for work, and I was often left with relatives. I especially loved staying with my great-grandparents. Their home was spotless, filled with little treasures I couldn't resist touching, and they were always so kind to me.

The last place I lived with my biological parents and younger brother, a boy about two years my junior, was a tiny, run-down house with threadbare carpet and old pull-down shades. Out front stood a big tree with a tire swing. I'd play on it for hours, waiting eagerly for my father to come home. I couldn't wait to see him.

But we weren't there for long. Eventually, my brother and I were sent to stay with a kind relative, where I felt safe. Then one day, I was told my brother would remain with them, while another family was adopting me. Though they were also relatives, I didn't know who they were. Years later, I was told we'd met before, but I had no memory of it. At the time, I was terrified. Would I ever see my brother again? The uncertainty shook me. That night, I couldn't sleep. I lay awake crying, watching my brother as he slept beside me.

"Brother, I hope you have a good life," I whispered. "I'll try to come back for you."

At four, I was adopted, given a new name, and told to call my new parents Mom and Dad. They cared for me and gave me a life of hard-earned privilege, one I remain deeply grateful for. Still, I ached for my little brother and my biological parents. God, I missed them so much.

Always the outsider in the new family, I never could figure out where I stood with one of the family members; communication between us was difficult at best. From day one and throughout my life, I had to walk on eggshells around that person.

Our interaction remained a continuous stressor until, eventually, there were no more eggshells to break.

Year after year, it became increasingly difficult for me to articulate my goals, dreams, and mostly my fears to my adoptive parents. Many times, I have found myself stuttering and struggling to recall specifics when discussing stressful issues.

I was frequently dismissed or misunderstood as an overly sensitive child. "What happens in life is just life," I was told, which made me increasingly insecure and shy throughout the years. Not being able to talk and having to hide events in my life from family and friends made it extremely difficult for me to process and manage my emotions from day to day. At around the age of six, I believed that if I worked harder, it would open the door to communication with my family. At that time, I didn't know that giving it my heart and soul would still leave it a painful, unreachable goal in my life.

My stepdad was a workaholic; it was common for him to work ten to twelve hours a day, seven days a week, and to be gone for months at a time working in the bush. By around age ten, I compared myself to him and considered myself somewhat lazy. That concerned me because I didn't want him or his employees to see me as a bum. So, in my mind, I had to redouble my efforts and try to work twice as hard as any of his employees to avoid embarrassing him. After all, he was my hero.

My stepparents were very good people, but the lack of communication tends to fade hope, no matter how much one tries. Fortunately, I made a friend in Kiana to play with: a big German shepherd named King. Our family friend Larry's mom owned the dog and kept it tied up in the back of her house in a small alley-like area. He was the greatest thing in the world to me at that time. Maybe more so than the cookies; yes, much more. I could hide out and play with that dog for hours. We had so much fun together. He truly was a good companion. Many times, I tried to sneak up on him, but as I'd peer around the corner, I would see King standing up at attention, waiting to play with me. How did he know it was me coming around the corner?

"Hi, King! How's my buddy today?" I would say in a playful voice.

Out of his mouth would come a long, pink tongue as he leaped toward me and up onto my chest. I would try to get him off, but he'd pin me to the ground and lick my face.

"Off! Off, boy! Off King! Come on now, get off," I'd happily cry out. I was a skinny kid who weighed around eighty-five pounds at that time, and I am sure King weighed at least seventy-five pounds plus. Because of his size and strength, it was tough for me to keep such a beast in control.

Happiness seemed to glow all around him, except when the Native kids walked near him. Then, he would drop his head and push his ears forward, glaring, and his lips would lift, exposing his sharp white teeth. He would lunge forward at the children until the fifteen- to twenty-foot steel leash stretched out. His leash was the only thing that stopped him from pouncing on the children. He continued to bark and stretch the leash until he was standing on his hind legs, pawing as if he wanted a piece of them. Wow, I mean, this dog was mad, almost out of control.

"King! Down, boy! Get down!" I'd shout to him.

The kids looked pale as they passed by King's domain. Larry's mom told me some children were mean to King, throwing rocks and hitting him with sticks. No wonder King seemed upset with them. I was glad that King liked me from the start. He never growled at me. After the kids left, King quickly calmed down and started to play with me.

"King, I have to go to work now. I will see you later," I said on this particular morning.

As I made my way through the alley, turning left up the dirt road toward one of the new houses I was to help build, I could see the plumber was busy working.

"Hey, James, how's it going?" I asked.

"OK, I'm working on the plumbing trees," James replied.

"Can I help?"

I was a kid who minded adults. I took orders well and was willing to work hard. I could only do so much at that age, given my size and weight. However, I was more than willing to learn and work around my limitations. I was fascinated by the idea of connecting pipes and then filling them with water to detect any leaks. The plumber, a Vietnam veteran, was a soft-spoken, burly guy with a beard. When he spoke, you had to listen carefully. He seemed gentle, but crossing him might be dangerous. I liked him, and he was good to me, so out of respect, when James asked me to do something, I did it, even if I disliked some of the chores I was doing for him.

"You want to sand the pipes for a while?" he asked.

"Sure. How much?" I questioned.

"We have all these villages to do. There's a lot of work in front of us, and all of the ends of the pipes need to be cleaned so I can solder them." "OK, sure, where do I start?" I enthusiastically responded.

There were many sizes and thicknesses of copper pipe, ranging from three-quarters of an inch to four inches, scattered throughout. James also pre-cut the pipes for the boiler system and put those into separate piles.

I straddled a stool, placed the thick copper pipe between my legs, and started to sand. The type of sandpaper I used was called plumber's cloth, a strong material. I sat hunched over on a bucket, sanding pipes all day. Eventually, my wrists were aching, and my hands went numb, but I didn't mind. I was doing important work. I believed I was making a difference; after all, the plumbing we worked on would be used for years to come. It was me sanding the joints and making sure they were sanded well so that when James soldered them together, they would not leak.

While sanding, I could hear James cutting pipes, making many more piles of pipes for me to sand. At the end of the day, I could see I hadn't even made a dent. *Oh man, this is going to be a lot of work.* I took pride in sanding those plumbing trees, hour after hour, day after day, rain or shine, sanding, always sanding while my fingers and wrists were cramped and constantly aching.

I saw James applying flux to the joints and soldering the copper pipes. I was proud to see all of those pieces fit together. It was like a big jigsaw puzzle.

The plumbing tree was a sanitary loop (sewer line) that fit into the plumbing wall. We assembled the plumbing trees in one location for all the homes.

Once in a while, James let me cut the pipes. I really got a thrill out of that. He showed me how to measure the pipe correctly and use the manual pipe cutter safely. To use the pipe cutter, I had to hold one end of the copper pipe with my left hand while spinning the pipe cutter with my right hand and twisting the threaded cutting mechanism. This would take many rotations and twisting before the pipe was cut. Obviously, it was much easier to cut the three-quarters than the four-inch pipe. Cutting the four-inch pipe was much trickier because both the pipe and the cutting device were large and heavy. It took a lot of my strength and energy to cut the pieces. When I finally cut through the first piece, I heard the excess copper clank on the ground.

"James, these trees are looking great," I said with pride.

"Yeah, if they don't leak," he said under his breath.

"When will you install them?" I asked.

"I think the first house will be ready tomorrow," he said with a smirk. I promised myself I would join him, so I went to bed early that night.

Getting to sleep during the summer months in Alaska can be challenging due to the sunlight streaming into bedrooms. However, the Arctic Circle proved to be even more difficult. You have to do everything possible to block out the light, and curtains may not be sufficient to do so. I have seen people tape foil and paper on their windows. Fortunately, the sunlight never bothered me because I was always tired from the day's work.

I bunked with James, and he would often yell at someone in his sleep. Many nights, he had woken me up by crying out, "Come to me, come to me, it's OK."

"James, are you OK?" I would ask.

"Go back to sleep, don't worry about it," he always told me.

It did worry me. I think he was having nightmares about the Vietnam War. I don't know, but that's what it seemed like.

The next day, I got up early because I wanted to help James install the first plumbing tree, but he had already left. I threw on my pants and wolfed down breakfast without even brushing my teeth.

"Slow down, David. Why are you in a rush?" Rhoda asked.

I had to go to the store and help some of the other crews with tools and materials before I could help James. It took me some time to run those damn errands, so I ran from place to place all around the village. Later that morning, I finally made my way to the first house. It was easy to find because it sat on a V-shaped lot, and I would walk by it whenever I went to the river to fish or help out with supplies. I was so proud of what my stepfather was accomplishing. I kept thinking about how much these magnificent buildings would help the local people.

All was quiet outside, and I didn't see James. I wondered where he was. The plumbing and other construction materials were scattered under the house, protected from the morning's rain.

Maybe he's inside installing the plumbing tree, I thought, but I didn't hear any noise from inside the house either. It started pouring rain as I made my way up the stairs, so I was hoping to work indoors until the rain stopped. *Hope King stays dry.*

I negotiated my way around the materials and tools, careful not to step on protruding nails that pierced boards and other miscellaneous objects.

For the most part, the work crews maintained good housekeeping, ensuring the job sites remained clean. After I reached the top of the stairs, I found James.

"Hey James, it looks like you installed the first plumbing tree without me," I said, my voice filled with excitement.

"Yeah, check it out," he said. He had already been working on the other plumbing systems, and now he was installing the plumbing for the heating system.

Wow, man, he's fast. It's not even nine o'clock, I thought, as I closely examined the plumbing tree.

Due to my stepdad's brilliant, well-thought-out design, James could slide the copper plumbing tree between the stud walls, giving easy access to it. "Your dad sure makes my job easier," James commented.

Very cool stuff!

I continued to help him for the rest of the day and was happy to do so, as I didn't want to go out in the rain. After a long day of work, the rain finally subsided, and the sun shone brightly in the evening sky. I was tired, but it was nice outside, and I wanted to catch some fish while I still had some energy. I figured I would go after dinner and take some extra cookies with me. My fishing pole was usually rigged for whitefish and ready to go. I have always eaten very fast since I was a little child; that's just the way I was. After dinner, I grabbed my fishing pole and tackle box and ran down to the river, but not before saying hi to King.

Seeing the Kobuk River from the top of the village was beautiful, and I couldn't wait to catch some fish. The dirt road from the top of the hill to the river was fairly steep. I mean, three-wheelers and vehicles could drive up and down the road, but it was still a steep hill, and walking up it was not much fun, especially if you were carrying items. That hill took my breath out, even though I was young. A gravelly sandbar that ran perpendicular to the river is where I did most of my fishing. Many of the villagers' boats were parked on that sandbar, including my stepfather's floatplane.

The location was near the home where we stayed. I often went there several times a day or night, allowing me to meet up with him when he flew in for the day. He used Kiana as a base camp and flew to the other villages daily to check on the rest of the housing projects.

I usually caught whitefish from that sandbar, but once in a while, I caught Arctic grayling and Arctic char. Grayling and trout were my favorite fish to catch, especially graylings, because they are great little fighters and are very tasty. Catching each species of fish was a challenge in their own way. That night, I was mainly going after whitefish. They were fun, great fighters, and relatively easy to hook. I loved being up late on a sunny night, gazing at the river with my pole line in the water, watching the birds fly, and listening to the sounds of the river. Gazing out in the distance, I kept thinking I had stepped back in time.

I didn't keep most of the fish I caught. My stepdad was vastly knowledgeable about the outdoors and had taught me conservation at an early age. He told me from time to time, "We have to protect the animals, put them back in the wild, so the next time we come out and want to go fishing, they will be there. Maybe you'll even catch the same fish." I have followed that rule to this day. The fish were running hot that evening. I caught and released a bunch without injuring a single one.

Days later, late in the afternoon, I was playing in the bunkhouse where some of the crew stayed. There was an old stereo and some large windows, and I was having fun, minding my own business and doing childish things. Flies would land on a window, and I would sneak up to them and, using my middle finger, flick them off the window. I wasn't trying to kill them, but simply knock them down. After they fell to the floor, I'd bend down and blow on them; suddenly, they'd wake up and fly away unharmed.

I had done that a couple of times when I faintly heard a lady calling for help.

What's going on? I wondered.

As I approached the front window, I could see a woman walking toward the front of the house. Something about her was not right.

"Help me! Help me! Please! Help me!" she cried out.

What? What is that?

I could feel my heart beating faster and faster. My legs started to shake, and my body tightened up.

What is going on?

The woman continued to walk slowly toward me.

What should I do? I don't know what to do. Oh God, please help me. What should I do?

I ran to the front door. Time seemed to stand still. I moved in slow motion. As I reached for the doorknob, I could see my hand visibly shaking.

Oh my God! I've got to open this door.

"Help me, please, help me!" she continued to cry out.

I purposely stared at the ground as I opened the front door, too frightened to look up. Still looking down while descending the porch stairs toward her, I finally worked up enough nerve and slowly looked up at her. She uttered in a weak voice, "Help me! Help me!"

I was horrified. I could not believe my eyes! *Oh my God! Please, no. Oh my God! Please, no.* I was gasping for air and could barely speak. The hair on the back of my head felt like it was standing straight up. *No, please, no!* "Help me, please! I need help," she exclaimed.

She was a short, thin woman. Her face was pale, and I will never forget her eyes. She stared at me with those dead eyes. It seemed she was looking right through me. It was strange and it scared the wits out of me. As a fourteen-year-old child, I had never seen so much blood and carnage. It took a lot of effort not to puke my guts out. It was horrible, simply horrible beyond belief.

She was covered in blood. Blood was everywhere. Her hair, covered in blood, was matted to her skull. Blood was dripping into her eyes, mouth, and ears, onto her arms, hands, and shoes. Her clothes were drenched in blood.

Oh God, no! I shouted in my head. *No, no, no!*

Blood was spraying from the side of her head in long, thin spurts. Spurt after spurt, blood sprayed as much as two to three feet away from her erect body, hitting the dirt road. The blood bounced off the fine, powdery dirt, raising tiny plumes of dust while blood droplets splashed back on the ground and her feet and legs.

"Help me! Help me!" she cried out.

I had no clue what to do.

"It will be all right," I told her. I could barely talk, let alone get help.

"Help me, please help me," she kept crying out in a broken voice.

"Oh, OK, hang on," I replied.

Trying to avoid her blood continuing to spray out of the right side of her head, I finally got up close to her despite feeling nauseous at the sight.

Oh God! Dad, help me! Even though my biological father had passed away, I always asked him for guidance and protection. I shouted as I ran toward the first house where we installed the plumbing tree. I saw the work crews coming toward us from the corner of my eye.

"Help! Help! There's a lady bleeding! Help!" I shouted to the workers. My mind was spinning. Seeing all that blood made me want to throw up. The next thing I remember, I was standing on the riverbank next to my stepdad's Cessna 185 floatplane, watching this poor lady being boarded. Someone had wrapped her head in bandages, which didn't help much. Blood was completely soaked through the bandages. She looked like a bloody mummy. My stepdad was frantically helping her into the airplane. I am not sure if he was able to do a pre-flight check because he was in such a rush to get this woman to the nearest hospital, which was in Kotzebue. I just stood behind the airplane, shaking.

As I looked up toward the hill, I saw a little boy around four or five years old standing near me, crying and shaking.

"Mommy, mommy," he cried out.

Later that day, I was told the child had witnessed the vicious beating and stabbing of his mother.

"Mommy, mommy," he kept crying out.

I could hardly breathe. The white and green Cessna 185 was parked on the water, tied to the shore like a boat. I untied the plane and pushed it out into the water. I heard the fuel pump winding up, then the starter grinding as the propeller rotated, followed by the roar of the 300- horse-power engine coming to life. The propeller blast and exhaust hit my face, and the cool wind blew around me.

As soon as it was safe, my stepfather turned the aircraft into the wind and applied full throttle for takeoff. The floatplane rocked back and forth on the Kobuk River. The piercing sound of the powerful engine was almost deafening. The aircraft quickly got on the step, and before I knew it, he was in the air, flying this poor woman to the hospital.

As I stood there, watching the airplane fly off into the horizon, I wondered why this was happening. I turned around and saw the boy crying out for his mother, tears were running down his face. I was hoping the woman would survive, but it seemed pretty doubtful due to all of the blood she had lost. Plus, it takes about twenty-five minutes to fly to Kotzebue.

The Kobuk River was moving gracefully, the birds were flying, and wildlife in its entire splendor seemed untouched, as though nothing had happened. I guess nature has a way of absorbing pain. I knew the earth itself could not feel, but humans sure can. I suppose that is what makes life so hard for each of us.

As I walked toward the cliffs of Kiana, I noticed a small to medium; sized rock. I sat on it and stared over the beautiful, peaceful Kobuk River. I don't know how long I sat on that rock. I just sat there and stared out, asking myself why.

In this stressful situation, I thought about my father, Gordon. I had only heard whispers about the kind of guy he was, but he was my dad, and I fondly remember the glimpses I had of him. I remember having fun every time I saw him. He would speed up and drive faster under the underpasses in his red convertible as we laughed together. I remember his laugh. I missed him so much! After the adoption, I had no contact with him.

Sometime during the summer of 1972, when I was seven, my father died. A person who shall remain unnamed told me that he had killed himself because he couldn't live without my brother and me. I blamed myself for his death. I felt a great deal of sadness and guilt that overwhelmed and robbed me of trust in one adult in particular, who was supposed to protect children.

Dad, I wish you were still alive. I miss you. I hope you are in heaven and that everything is well with you. Help me, please. I need somebody to talk to. I don't want to see any more violence.

I hung around for a while, waiting for my stepfather to get back. I was hoping that the woman would be OK. I remember my body going numb and that numbness was almost unbearable. The next thing I remember was petting King in the alley. I seemed to have lost time. I tried to sleep that night, but every time I closed my eyes, there she was. The pale-faced lady kept coming closer and closer to me as though it were a repeated pattern.

Her eyes were a dull white, and the clothes she was wearing were soaked with blood dripping toward the ground. Blood was spraying and oozing out of her head, completely covering her face, hands, and feet. A constant thin spray of blood was spurting out of the side of her head and splashing all over the fine, powdery dirt. "Help me, please help me," she cried out over and over again, and I could see the little boy crying out for his mommy. The endless images seemed so real. I got sick to my stomach seeing those images in my mind. I wanted them to go away. I tried to sleep.

I had no one to talk to about this event. I was told, "That's just life," but it was hard for me to compartmentalize what had happened. I think even the strongest minds would have a hard time coming to terms with something as horrible as that. I mean, how in the hell is a child supposed to deal with witnessing that type of violence?

The next day, after a restless night, I lay in bed and didn't feel like getting up. I wanted to stay in a place that seemed somewhat safe. I wanted to stay there as long as possible before entering the cruel real world. I don't remember eating that day, but I did go to work without discussing what I had seen the day before with anyone.

A couple of days later, after a hard day's work, I overheard a conversation in which the woman's husband had brutally attacked her. Apparently, she and her husband had been drinking that day, which confused me because the villages were supposed to be dry, which meant no alcohol was allowed. At that time, Kotzebue was the only town where people could access liquor. I was told that her husband had beaten her and whacked her in the head many times with an ulu in front of the little boy.

An ulu is a curved all-purpose knife traditionally used by Native Americans. A small handle is mounted at the center of the blade. The handle is made of either wood, bone, or ivory. It was my understanding that the metal for the blade was cut and shaped from old hand saws, similar to the ones you would find at your local hardware store. Ulus are versatile and efficient, sharp tools that can be used to skin and clean animals, cut hair, and even trim blocks of snow and ice used to build igloos. I doubt the inventor meant ulus to harm human beings.

To everyone's surprise, the woman did indeed survive. *Thank God.* Nobody knows for sure how she lived through that horrible ordeal, especially considering all of that blood loss. I had heard that because she'd consumed so much alcohol, it may have saved her life. It is ironic how something so destructive can preserve life. She must have been very drunk to be able to handle all of the pain from the deep, penetrating wounds. To my knowledge, she never filed any charges against her husband. I would have, but who am I to judge?

I felt terrible for the little boy who witnessed his mother being savagely attacked by his father. I wondered how he would be able to handle that horrible event in his mind. *I'm shocked by what I saw, but Jesus, how is he dealing with it? I just don't know.*

As it turns out, I would endure long-lasting struggles of trying to come to terms with what I'd seen.

CHAPTER 6
Remote Hazards

"The fire department and ambulance have arrived," said the officer.

Thank God! Finally, I will be getting out of here. Now if they can just get this steering wheel off me. I can still wiggle my toes. That's good. I am not paralyzed yet.

I wondered how close I was to not being able to use my feet or my legs. My bloody left hand was still hanging out the front window. I couldn't move my hand, but I wasn't too concerned about it. My mind was mostly focused on my legs and feet and just trying to breathe. As I wheezed and struggled to get air into my lungs, I could hear sirens and people talking in the background. I could see the flashing red and blue lights from the vehicles.

Oh yes! They are here, it's true. Soon, I will be released from this steel cage. I am pinned like a trapped animal.

Things were a little blurry. What happened to the windshield? Did it shatter on impact? Or did they cut it away from me? *Strangely, I didn't remember seeing any glass around me. Even though the windshield was made with safety glass, I was sure there had to be glass everywhere. I just didn't know where.*

I struggled to breathe. At times, getting oxygen in and out of my lungs felt like an eternity.

Damn, I am not going to pull through. No way, not a chance.

I was sure I was about to suffocate. That is, if I didn't freeze to death first.

"We'll have you out of here soon," the police officer said.

"Cold, I am cold, very cold."

MOST PRE- AND YOUNG TEENS don't have to contend with the violence that was commonplace in the bush. On the other hand, most kids don't get to co-pilot planes. Working in the bush gave me firsthand experience with heavy equipment, airplanes, boats, barges, and even helicopters. Wow, who wouldn't like that?

My stepfather's company flew around fourteen million pounds of materials from Anchorage International Airport to north of the Arctic Circle. I was told it was the biggest airlift in Alaska at the time. I don't know, but many claimed that to be true. He used a variety of aircraft types, including the Short SC.7 Skyvan, C-119s, Aviation Traders ATL-98 Carvair, which resembled a 747 with propellers, and numerous other types of aerial transportation.

These aircraft were so old that the pilots and mechanics jokingly called them "flying coffins." Heck, they even added a jet engine on top of the C-119s, not for safety, but because the radial engines lacked sufficient thrust to take off due to the weight of the materials. Even if that was not enough, they injected water into the cylinders to increase the thrust by as much as 30% on takeoff. Yeah, risky, you bet it was. Once the materials were dropped off at the village airport or arrived by barge, a UH-34D Seahorse helicopter carried the materials, slinging the load underneath and flying it to the remote lot sites.

As a kid, I helped load planes with plywood, foundation pads, roofing metal, and various construction materials in Anchorage. While working up north, I flew in a helicopter to other villages, such as Selawik, and worked with the pilot to stage the same materials that I'd assisted in sending from Anchorage.

Once the materials arrived, the pilot navigated the craft toward the materials and hovered overhead, dangling a sling within arm's reach of the handler below. The handler securely hooked the materials to the sling and signaled to the pilot that the cargo was secured. After the pilot acknowledged all was well, he'd slowly and carefully climb vertically to avoid hitting other objects and fly to the designated lot.

Once over the lot, the pilot carefully set the cargo down to avoid damaging the materials and then released the hook, allowing the sling to drop. A worker on the ground would walk on the lumpy tundra toward the slings and prepare them to hook back up to the helicopter. The pilot then returned and hovered over the person within arm's reach, and they would reach up and hook one end of the sling to the helicopter. The pilot would slowly rise straight up, sliding the slings out from underneath the cargo, and then return and get the next cargo. The process was repeated all day until the barges or the staging ground were empty.

Someone designated me to be a handler on the lots. It was exciting and fun, but at the same time, it gave me pause because those big old piston-driven helicopters used in Vietnam were now hovering over my head. They were not equipped with a reliable jet engine. A jet engine is about 117 times less likely to fail than a piston engine. So, there's that. I wasn't some overly sensitive kid needlessly worrying about being under a helicopter hovering just above my head at arm's length.

Even at that age, I knew quite a bit about the reliability of piston engines. Before leaving California, my uncle taught me how small and large vehicle engines work, as well as how to repair and rebuild them. I knew a great deal about how they worked. I kept thinking, what if that old piston engine quits? I mean, you should hear what it sounds like when it starts up. To me, there seemed to be nothing airworthy on that helicopter from my point of view. How do you escape if it starts to fall out of the sky while hovering over your head? Believe me, it's not as easy as you think. It's a gigantic machine, hovering just over your head, so what direction do you run? Wind direction and speed were factors. Are you fast enough to escape the length of the chopper and add in the long rotor blades? Those things were huge; there is no escape. Oh, let's not forget trying to run on the lumpy tundra. I knew I could be dog meat if that chopper had a mishap over my head.

When it rained, the rotor tips produced static electricity, which traveled down to the metal hooks. While hooking or unhooking the slings, I would sometimes get shocked. The shock was unpleasant, and it hurt most of the time. Come to think of it, I did not want to do that task while it was raining, and I never did again. Lesson learned.

In addition to being a handler, I was tasked with fueling the helicopter. Because the helicopter could only lift a certain amount of weight, I was allocated fifty-five gallons of fuel, which weighed approximately 330 pounds each time the pilot landed. The helicopter's gross weight was put to its limits. The pilot would have to land and refuel every couple of trips, and I would run back and forth between the lots and the helicopter to refuel. As tired as I was, I was grateful that the fuel pump was battery-powered, unlike the old hand pumps.

I did learn one more thing about helicopters. One winter, the helicopter pilot demonstrated that it was possible to make a snowball and throw it up through the rotating rotors, and it would not hit the rotors due to the airfoil effect. Seeing that trick was fascinating. We'd catch the snowballs when they came down between the rotors.

While working in Selawik, I went fishing on an outboard boat. I met a very nice elderly gentleman who was retired. I don't know what he was doing way north, but he had a houseboat, and I followed him all over Lake Selawik to catch fish. Our goal was to catch a large Northern Pike. To my surprise, his ultimate goal was to eat one because he wanted to know what it tasted like. Yuck, I thought, how gross. Later that day, he fried up a pike he caught, which did not look too appetizing to me. The meat looked mushy and had a yellowish tint. Plus, it was full of tiny bones. Thanks, but no thanks. I wasn't going to eat that fish. No way. Maybe if I were starving, I would have, but believe me, I wasn't hungry enough that day.

The wind was dead calm, and the lake lay flat. However, it was raining buckets, and the mosquitoes were brutal, even in the middle of the lake during a downpour. There was no escape. Somehow, they're able to fly during the hardest rain. Mosquitoes are particularly nasty during the rain because every time you spray on mosquito repellent, the rain washes it off your body. That leaves you with no protection, and they attack with extreme prejudice. Not only can they fly during the pouring rain, but they also chase you around small and large lakes. At thirty-one miles long and around six to eight miles wide, Lake Selawik is the third-largest lake in Alaska.

I have heard that mosquitoes kill people, and I believe it. They are the vampires of the north. Getting attacked by these little insects can cause a person to lose their mind, run into lakes, and drown. No matter where you go, they find you. While fishing, I cast out a couple of times, and they somehow found me and immediately attacked me. I would rush, start the motor, and drive as fast as possible to another spot on the lake, casting out two or three times, only to get attacked; then I would drive as fast as I could to another place to fish. I would do this all day. Talk about persistent hunters. I asked myself how these little bastards can travel so far from the shoreline. Wouldn't they be too tired to suck your blood? Nature is amazing, and learning to survive in Alaska's remote areas was a valuable lesson.

And boy, were we remote! Much of Alaska is accessible only by airplane because the road system is nonexistent. I often would go out to the river and listen to the sound of my stepdad's engine. I was familiar with his white and green Cessna 185 because he purchased the airplane when we first moved to Alaska. Usually, 185s sound about the same in the air, but for some reason, his plane had a unique whiny pitch. No one could tell us why his engine sound was so distinctive, but my uncle and I could always identify it as his plane, even when it was out of sight.

He had the first floatplane north of the Arctic Circle because he needed to use it for work. 185's can be fitted with wheels, skis, or floats and are equipped with a 300-horsepower power plant. During takeoff, the propeller tips break the sound barrier, creating a distinctive, piercing roar that's impossible to mistake.

When we first moved to Alaska, he used that same 185 floatplane to transport building materials for a cabin we built on Trapper Lake, about thirty minutes north of Anchorage. We loaded many different types of construction materials and supplies into the aircraft, from two-by-six studs, nails, and insulation to just about everything you need to build a house except for the plywood and the boat. Because of their large size, he had to hire a larger aircraft, known as a Beaver, and strap those items to the outside of the floats.

We would take off from Spenard Lake in Anchorage, fly north for about thirty minutes, and land on the lake near the cabin's location. We would fly back and forth all day, loading and unloading the materials onto the shore. Then, I would pack the materials up a fifteen-foot semi-cliff to the cabin site. It was a great time because it allowed me to spend time with my stepfather and learn about aviation.

He wasn't the only person I flew with. A friendly, heavyset man with a round face named Jimmy worked as a pilot for my stepdad, who'd recently purchased a Cessna 207 to fly his crews, supplies, and building materials to the villages. Airplanes were a crucial tool for his business; a costly and risky asset to manage, especially in the unforgiving terrain of rural Alaska.

Jimmy had flown helicopters in Vietnam and was instrument-rated in them, which was a difficult rating to acquire. He told me stories of flying around the great pyramids in Egypt. How cool is that! However, my stepfather had reservations about hiring him. As talented as Jimmy was, and despite having multiple highly sought-after air ratings, he was concerned that Jimmy might take too many unintentional chances and crash or overtax the airplanes, which could result in him incurring more maintenance and replacement costs, not to mention the risk to lives. I think that after a lengthy discussion, he received some reassurances from Jimmy that he would not take any risks and would not overstress the aircraft's design limits.

In my second summer working in the bush, I was based in Kotzebue. Luckily for me, Jimmy was flying out of Kotzebue, delivering construction materials for the new housing project in multiple villages short hops. Once my long workday was over, I would walk to the commercial jet airport, meet him, and help him load the airplane. If I was lucky, he would let me fly with him. Most of the time, I got lucky.

During this trip, we were tasked with delivering foundation materials and supplies. We loaded heavy, pressure-treated foundation boards three inches thick, eight inches wide, and four feet long. We brought 50-penny spikes and some roofing screws. The aircraft had additional cargo space in front of the 207, behind the engine cowling. The plane is designed for seven seats, but we removed the seats, except for the pilot and copilot seats, to make room for the materials inside the plane, just like we did for the 185.

After the main section of the aircraft had been loaded, I noticed the tail was resting on the ground and the front steering tire was hanging in midair. There was barely enough room for us to get inside the plane. *We must be out of balance,* I thought, *since 207s have tricycle gear three wheels, two for the main wheels and one for steering. I guess we're not going to steer the aircraft to the runway.*

I asked the pilot if the plane would make it. Pilots are responsible for ensuring that cargo and passengers are correctly loaded. The aircraft mustn't exceed the weight and balance requirements recommended by the manufacturer. Exceeding those requirements can cause the plane to behave erratically during flight, which could lead to a crash.

"Don't worry," he said. "We still have to load the front compartment." *OK, that made sense to me.*

We added a lot of additional weight in the front, but the front wheel did not go down. I wondered if we were still out of balance and overloaded. Maybe after we both got on the plane, the nose would come down, and the steering gear wheel would touch the ground. After all, the pilot was a heavy man. *Would we be overloaded after we both got in,* I wondered. *Did he fly like this all the time?*

Even after we both settled into our seats, the aircraft's nose dropped slightly, but the front wheel did not touch the ground. I heard him say, "OK, Dave, ready? Seat belts on? Check?" He turned the key to start the engine. The engine cranked over as I saw the three-bladed propellers rotating clockwise. As the engine idled, the plane's front nose wheel finally dropped down, touching the tarmac. I was rightfully nervous because I believed the plane was out of balance and exceeded the gross weight limits. This brought back a memory of a similar situation that had shaken me up a couple of years back.

On one of our trips flying supplies to our cabin using the same Cessna 185, the weight and balance had exceeded the manufacturer's requirements. We had too much weight aft of the plane, which caused problems during landing. We bounced hard several times, on and off the water, and my stepfather struggled to keep the aircraft under control. Luckily, he was able to land the plane without incident. Had someone with less skill been flying, the outcome could have been fatal.

I hope everything is OK, I thought.

Jimmy started his pre-flight check. The engine gauges were already in the green from his previous flight. He let me taxi out to the paved runway; the sun was still above the horizon. Oh, what a beautiful sight! It should be smooth sailing with clear skies and calm winds. Cleared for takeoff, he pushed the throttle toward the firewall, and the engine came to life as the plane accelerated to around seventy miles per hour. He gently pulled back on the yoke, and the airplane lifted off the ground and into the air.

The 207 was a smooth-running and relatively quiet aircraft, even for a piston-driven engine. The three-bladed propeller reduced the engine's noise and vibration. I liked this plane because it had a turbocharged engine, which gave it more power. Plus, it had electric flaps and trim systems. It was an excellent airplane.

From our aerial vantage point, I could see rivers, lakes, and tundra, as well as mostly flat lands. I remember part of the terrain looked like a swamp with small bushes everywhere. Occasionally, we spotted moose with big antlers walking around. Of course, my favorite animals to see were swans. Swans are some of the most glorious creatures on God's green earth. I always loved flying over lakes and seeing swans swimming around. These great birds add such beauty to the vastness of Alaska. Swans are known to mate for life. Usually, two swans can be seen together.

It was a smooth flight. I just sat back and took it all in, looking down at the green terrain and winding rivers. It seemed most of the state's millions of lakes were north of the Arctic Circle. We saw lake after lake. Looking down at the lakes and rivers, I could see the sun's bright reflection bouncing off the water. What a sight! Sometimes, I swear the landscape did not seem real; it looked more like a painting. On the other hand, beauty can be deceiving. I could hear my grandpa saying in my head, "A land without mercy." You must be tough to survive the vastness of nature in this state.

As I turned to the right side of the aircraft window, I could see the fowl migration heading south. Such a sight! It seemed like thousands of birds were flying. Now, they are the smart ones. Humans can learn a great deal from birds and animals in general if we take the time to observe them closely. They are heading toward the heat. *Oh, lucky them*, I thought. *They come up north for the summer for the good life and head south for the winter for the other good life.*

Sometimes, if we were lucky, we would see magnificent, blond grizzly bears. From above, you can see their hair moving in waves like tall grass blowing in the wind, and their muscles ripple with each step. Man! They are huge. Big and powerful, they can run up to forty-nine miles per hour in a short burst. They can easily walk or run on the dry or swampy tundra and swim; they are a sight to behold. They say a bear can walk as much as twenty to forty miles a day looking for food.

A Native friend of ours once told me that a bear is left-handed, so if he takes a swing at you, try to roll with it, and you might survive. I don't know if they are left-handed, but I never wanted to tangle with a bear to find out.

The pilot interrupted my bear-related daydreaming. "Hey Dave, coming up to the first village. Get set, give me ten degrees of flaps."

This nice man would let me fly the plane toward our destination and instruct me on how many flaps to extend for our descent. Flaps on an aircraft change the aerodynamic shape of the wings. They move up or down depending on how the pilot wants the aircraft to perform. We used the flaps like an air brake to slow the airplane down for landing.

"Ten degree flaps," he said again.

At the same time, he pulled the throttle back, and I felt the aircraft slow down. Looking straight out in front, the runway was rapidly coming into view. Off to the side, I noticed many new houses being erected.

It looked like they were making good progress.

Cool, I thought. *I've never seen this village before.*

"More flaps," the pilot directed.

While I pushed the electric flap handle down to the second notch, he slowed the airplane down and slightly reduced power.

"Short final," the pilot said.

Just before touchdown, he pulled the nose up, flaring the aircraft to land. There was a slight squeak, and the main wheels touched the gravel runway. The airplane did not skip. To my relief, he made a smooth, safe landing.

After the engine was off, we immediately jumped out of the aircraft and the nose of the plane rose, with the front wheel suspended high above the ground. The pilot opened the front cargo door and pulled out a couple of boxes of roofing screws, and unloaded some foundation pads from the rear of the airplane. To my relief, the front wheel dropped down, touching the runway. I was thrilled that we had lightened the load, and the plane was back in balance. As a result, my nervousness went away, and I was excited to fly to the next village.

"OK, let's go," the pilot said.

"Where are we going?" I asked.

"To Kivalina."

"Oh, that village is on the ocean," I said.

"Yeah. Wait until you see the runway. It's pretty neat," the pilot said.

"Ready to take off?"

After lining up with the gravel runway, the pilot pushed the throttle toward the firewall. I could see the rpm gauge climbing. The engine loudly roared. We started to roll forward, accelerating to takeoff speed.

Gravel runways tend to create more drag on the aircraft's wheels, which can increase the distance required for takeoff. Even though our runway was gravel, the airplane was now lighter, and we were in the air much quicker, using less runway than at the Kotzebue airport. I noticed the pilot continued running the engine at full power much longer than my stepfather did. Each pilot has their own style of flying. My stepdad would apply full power, and within seconds after takeoff, he would pull back the power until the needles were in the green. I asked him why he throttled back like that. His answer was short and sweet. He said to save the engine, which is expensive to repair or replace. However, some pilots prefer to hang on the prop to gain altitude as quickly as possible before reducing power. There's nothing wrong with that, of course. Getting the plane as high off the ground before reducing the power is smart, but it does add more wear and tear to the engine.

Flying in Alaska is inherently dangerous, but flying north of the Arctic Circle, especially during that time, carries even greater risks. Pilots must navigate vast stretches of tundra, lakes, rivers, swamps, dense forests, and rugged mountains, often in extreme weather and far from any form of civilization. If the aircraft experiences mechanical issues, finding a safe place to land can be extremely difficult. And if you survive the crash, you're faced with a new set of threats: dehydration, injury, starvation, wild animals (including relentless mosquitoes), and unforgiving weather, to name a few.

I heard that the insurance company told my stepfather that, due to the many hours and high miles he had flown north of the Arctic Circle, statistically, he was supposed to be dead. I was shaken up and sad to hear he was living on borrowed time. I had already lost one father, and now I might lose another. On top of that, I'd recently witnessed the bloody woman he saved by flying her to Kotzebue. My stepfather was my hero, whom I admired and loved very much. I never talked to him or anyone about what I'd heard, but I carried my concern for his safety close to my chest for decades.

I knew then and there that I would never be a commercial pilot. No way! Never. I studied and worked hard to get my private pilot's license before receiving my driver's license. At age fifteen, I soloed during spring before going out to the bush, but there was no way I would ever fly for hire.

I was not enthusiastic about flying through rough weather, but I did love to fly on calm, sunny days and at night. I'd always found it so peaceful and mystifying how beautiful the world looks from the air, and this trip was no exception. When we reached cruise level, the pilot finally pulled back on the power, and the plane flew like a dream.

Coming up on the shoreline, I could see the vast gravel beaches of the Arctic. The waves crashed on the shore trees, and branches were scattered everywhere. By the looks of it, landing on the beach would not be advisable, even from this altitude. Pilots land on the beaches, but we were in a tricycle plane designed for fairly good runways, unlike my stepfather's plane. Though he had floats on his 185, it could easily be converted to a taildragger by removing the floats and installing wheels. They have tougher landing gear and can take more abuse from hard landings. If the engine failed and we were forced to land on the beach, the landing gear could collapse from impact, and our chances of survival would be substantially reduced.

"Coming up on Kivalina," the pilot said.

Kivalina is a small village situated on the coast. It's got to be a cold place to live in the winter, but it was a pretty town with nice, warm, friendly people who live off the land to support themselves. A noble way of living. If you ask me, all the Native and non-Native people who live off the land are noble. Think about it for a minute. They reside in small, isolated villages with no roads connecting them to other villages, and the only way to reach them is by air. A person could acquire a snow machine, a boat, or a dogsled, but they are still in the middle of nowhere.

Many villages lack grocery stores or medical facilities. While it's true that some villages have medical clinics, they are not hospitals. People run the risk of medical emergencies, and if they're not able to receive proper care, they may die.

These villages used diesel or gas generators to produce electricity. What if they run out of fuel? You can't jump into your truck and get more fuel. How about water and sewer services? At that time, many villages had no running water or indoor plumbing. I've seen people carry five-gallon buckets of water from the riverbanks to their homes. During the winter, they would cut a hole in the ice, dip their buckets to fill them, and then carry the water back to their houses. Remember, the weather can drop to -60 degrees Fahrenheit, and the Arctic remains dark for extended periods. I've carried my fair share of water buckets in mid-winter, but I'll get to that later.

Satellite phones were used, but they were not entirely reliable. Cell phones had not been invented. It would be tough if someone were injured and couldn't call for help. I cannot emphasize enough how remote these villages are. That is why I have such great respect and admiration for these people.

A few minutes out, looking down at the shoreline, I could see what looked like a dead, headless walrus.

"Hey, what happened to the head?" I shouted.

The pilot told me that when a walrus carcass washes up on shore, it is usually because someone had taken its head to sell the ivory tusks. Walrus tusks are highly valued and worth a significant amount of money. Such a giant creature! I wouldn't want to come face-to-face with one of those great big animals.

"Coming up on Kivalina," the pilot said again. "Give me ten degree flaps, please."

Oh boy! My heart began to beat faster. I loved it. Doing something as simple as pressing the button down for ten degree flaps made me feel important. It seems silly, but I guess being asked to do little things feels significant when you are a kid.

"Hey, what's that?" I asked. "What kind of a runway is that?"

There was something about the surface. It looked like a normal runway, but it had a peculiar texture. The runway had several small holes in it.

"That's what I was trying to tell you," he said. "It's a metal airstrip. It's a good runway, very good. The military made many metal airstrips worldwide because the material was hard enough to land on, and it's cheap, efficient, and easy to install," the pilot said.

Wow! I thought. *I've never seen a metal airstrip before, let alone landed on one. This will be cool.*

The pilot pulled back the throttle.

"Give me full flaps," he said.

We were approximately 200 feet above ground and descending smoothly. I reached over, pushed down the electric flap handle, and smiled at the pilot, acknowledging that I had given him full flaps at the required time, a small job, but one that was essential. Looking around, I could see the ocean waves crashing on the shoreline. I was excited to see rocks and logs getting larger.

A slight bump and we were down just that fast. The runway felt a little bumpy, but overall, it was a flat surface. Caution was needed to avoid rolling off the end or to the side of the runway. Imagine being a pilot and getting stuck in the mud or sand while attempting to take off or land. I am sure that has happened to somebody.

After shutting off the aircraft, we jumped out. Unloading an aircraft always seemed easier than loading it, even though the timbers were just as heavy. We left the material at the side of the runway, and I didn't see anyone around. I began to sweat while unloading the plane. Once we were done, the pilot walked into the village for a few minutes and I sat down on the pilot's side of the main wheels. Suddenly, I felt cold. Man! Winter is coming! The seasons were changing so fast. I can hear my grandfather saying, "If you do not like the weather, wait five minutes." Oh boy! Was he ever right! Minutes passed, and I saw the pilot heading for the airplane, so I got up, opened the door, settled into the copilot's seat, and quickly fastened the seat belt tightly around my waist.

As the pilot settled in, I noticed out of the corner of my eye a beautiful red fox running into the tundra off the end of the runway. How cute these funny little creatures are! They are one of my favorite four-legged animals, a real gift from God. It is a thrill to see these animals in their natural habitat, untouched and wild.

Crank! Crank, the engine roared, and the pilot and I watched the gauges climb into the green. Once everything was green, the pilot maneuvered the aircraft and lined it up for takeoff. I love to monitor all the gauges.

"Ten degree flaps. Are you ready?" the pilot asked.

I applied the flaps, and the engine roared again. This time, taking off was much quicker. Removing cargo from the aircraft and burning off many gallons of fuel made the plane perform much better. Within seconds, we were in the air.

"Up flaps!" the pilot said.

I noticed him pulling back the power more quickly. He was a good pilot and knew what he was doing. Kotzebue, here we come!

Flying down the shoreline, I saw the same walruses lying on the beach. I felt sad while watching the migration of fowl again. *How lucky they were.* I wish I could travel with them. That would be the ultimate freedom. I wondered what life was like for them. Of course, I wouldn't want to be the duck or the goose getting shot at by some bird hunter.

When we were a few minutes away from Kotzebue, we encountered a strong crosswind and the pilot crabbed the aircraft into the wind.

Crabbing is a maneuver pilots do if the relative wind is causing the plane to veer off course. By turning the aircraft into the wind, the plane flies sideways while heading towards its destination.

"Ten degree flaps, please," the pilot said.

Oh, yeah! We are here, we've made it to Kotzebue. As we approached, I could see the runway just ahead.

"Ten degree flaps," I said.

Within minutes, we landed. The pilot reached over this time and flipped up the flap handle. As we slowly approached the tie-down, I could see the other aircraft wiggling even though they were tied down. The strong braided nylon ropes were holding, but I could see they were stretching. Even though the planes were tied down, they looked as if they were trying to fly. Why? It was strange and I didn't understand.

We finally pulled up to the tie-down, and the pilot turned off the engine. Quickly, he jumped out of the airplane and started to tie down the wing on his side. I rapidly started tying down the wing on my side. He didn't have to teach me how to secure the aircraft wing because I already had extensive experience. After tying down my side, I walked around the aircraft toward the tail. The pilot had beaten me to the punch and was tying down the rear of the plane.

"Hey, why do the planes act like they're flying when tied to the ground?"

"Whenever the wind is blowing over the leading edge of a wing, depending on how fast the air is moving, it can cause lift," he told me. "For example, an airplane can take off at forty miles an hour. If the wind blows forty miles an hour over a wing's leading edge, it creates lift on the wing."

"That's it?" I asked.

"Yeah, that's it," the pilot said. "Seems so simple, you know? In Anchorage, I've seen some big windstorms, trees blown down, roofs torn off, and airplanes flipped upside down, even when tied down." Now I knew why.

CHAPTER 7
Shots Fired

The officer got a blanket and placed it over me. I was still unable to move my body around. Hearing the metal being sheared off and seeing the cab come off the truck relieved me. I knew they would soon get the steering wheel off my chest.

Looking out of the corner of my left eye, I could see a man with a fireman's helmet walking toward me. I was going to be freed from this twisted heap!

"OK, we are going to get you out of here," the fireman said.

"You have to get this steering wheel off of me," I replied. "I can't breathe."

With my left eye, I could see him working on the door. What was the point of that? Given the circumstances, it was a weird question, especially since I was in so much pain, freezing cold, and tired. I had already been trapped in that truck for well over an hour. That is a long, long time to be stuck in one place fighting for your life.

KOTZEBUE LIES 26 miles north of the Arctic Circle and 549 miles northwest of Anchorage, situated on a narrow gravel spit roughly three miles long and just over half a mile wide. The land is treeless, dotted only with small shrubs. The climate is harsh and unforgiving, with temperatures remaining below freezing for more than two-thirds of the year. Annual precipitation is low, averaging around nine inches, while snowfall reaches approximately forty inches. For a brief period from early July to early October, Kotzebue Sound is free of ice. Even in summer, the average temperature rarely exceeds sixty degrees, as cold winds constantly blow off the Chukchi Sea. The sun barely sets in May, June, and July, making sleep difficult. Conversely, by December 21, the sun barely rises, providing only one hour and forty-one minutes of daylight.

I constantly asked myself how the Iñupiat Eskimos had adapted to such a relentless environment. They've lived here for roughly six centuries. Russian explorers were the first outsiders to arrive and trade for seal oil, skins, and furs. Eventually, whalers and gold seekers followed. Over time, Kotzebue became a vital hub, connecting ocean transport, inland river travel, and air access for the broader Northwest Arctic region. Goods, services, and fuel flowed through Kotzebue to smaller surrounding villages and nearby national parks like Kobuk Valley, Noatak Preserve, and the Bering Land Bridge. Due to its strategic location, it made sense for my stepdad to base his projects here, allowing him to reach nearby villages such as Kiana, where I had worked the previous summer.

The sky was overcast, and a cold rain came and went while my cousin Sam and I worked deep inside a large trench, knee-deep in icy, muddy water, installing sewer and water pipes. Sam was in his twenties, tall, lean, and serious—a man I respected. We wore hip waders to keep the freezing water from seeping in. As we sloshed around, I couldn't help but wonder why we had to work in such dangerous, remote places. I missed the sense of familiarity and safety that came with being home. I was fifteen, yet the violence and fear surrounding us had already left deep scars. I never shared the worst parts, even with close friends.

Most of my classmates back home had never been out to the bush. They couldn't relate to what I had seen or endured. By the time I returned each year, the gap between us grew. I kept quiet, bottling up the distress. As summer approached, anxiety gripped me, knowing I would be heading back out. I didn't know if I could make it through another season. I feared for my life every time we headed to the field.

The trench Sam and I were in towered above us. A ladder was the only way out. The backhoe had dug through the frozen ground. Shovels were useless against the permafrost. The operator's skill impressed me, as he maneuvered the machine with precision. Even though I knew trenching was dangerous work. I enjoyed watching the bucket swing, dig, and drop with grace. According to the Occupational Safety and Health Administration, excavation has about a 112 percent higher fatality rate than general construction work.[4]

Melting permafrost added to the hazard. Sunlight turned firm ground into slush. We used sump pumps constantly to keep the holes from flooding. Several times, cave-ins forced us to scramble out of the trench. We did have several cave-ins that had us rapidly climb out of the hole. Just one cubic yard of mud could weigh more than a car. If it collapsed on someone, they could be crushed. The cold only made things worse. Hypothermia was a constant threat.

We used urethane to seal the pipe joints and prevent freezing. I had seen it sprayed on houses as insulation, but for these joints, we mixed chemicals by hand in a bucket. The foam expanded and hardened quickly. Sam made sure every ounce was applied right—no waste, no shortcuts.

Once the insulation was cured, we backfilled the trench, carefully layering soil over the pipes. We did the first part by hand to avoid damaging them before the backhoe took over. I liked backfilling. It meant the job was nearly done, and the physical effort distracted me from darker thoughts.

That afternoon, we moved to a nearby house to fix a sewer line Sam had previously installed. He warned me, half-jokingly, about the old woman who lived there. "She might shoot at us," he said. I laughed nervously. I hoped it was just a joke.

We arrived and got to work. The ditch here was shallow and dry, a relief after the trench we had just escaped. I changed out of my waders into boots and grabbed tools from the truck. This job seemed manageable and might be completed by the end of the day.

My stepmom worked as a cook in Kotzebue, and she was an excellent cook. She put in grueling hours, up early and working late, seven days a week. Her food lifted the crew's spirits. She made things bearable in this isolated place.

Kotzebue had a bar and, surprisingly, a Dairy Queen, not something you'd expect that far north. The alcohol brought its own problems. Drinking was prevalent, and with that came more chaos.

"Hey, Dave, let's run some pipes," Sam said.

"OK," I replied. It felt good to focus on a straightforward task. I stayed close to Sam, which gave me a sense of security. I went back and forth from the truck, retrieving tools, mostly relying on my trusty round-point shovel. It was the better choice for hard ground.

Despite the cold, the aches in my hands and feet, I found something oddly satisfying about this work. Shoveling kept me busy. It was one of the few ways I could silence my mind. But I was beginning to notice my constant complaints. Maybe I'd always been that way. Perhaps the conditions were just that extreme.

Then something snapped, literally. A loud cracking noise. I ignored it at first. Maybe it was the equipment. I was digging again when I noticed men shouting and running. Then Sam yelled, "Dave, get down!"

I stared at him, confused. More cracking noises. Sam shouted again, louder this time, and sprinted toward me. He tackled me into the ditch, landing hard on top of me. More cracks, but this time I recognized them. Gunfire. Bullets zipped overhead with a high-pitched zing. I had heard guns before, but never bullets flying over my head, till now.

Sam covered me with his body, shielding me. I couldn't breathe; his weight pressed me into the dirt. The gunfire kept coming. Then, silence. He finally moved off, and I sat up, shaking. My mind spiraled. Visions of a woman's bloodied face and a child crying came flooding back. Flashbacks I couldn't escape. Sam had saved me, but the trauma burned itself into my memory.

I feel bad because I never told my family and his family how brave he was, willing to risk his life to save mine. And I don't remember if I properly thanked him before he passed away. God rest his soul.

That incident haunted me. I could never shake the image of the woman bleeding out or the crazy old lady shooting at us. The flashbacks followed me everywhere: school, home, even during downtime.

In class, I would suddenly be overwhelmed. I'd run to the bathroom and cry in a stall. I turned to TV and movies to escape the visions.

The memories were vivid, three-dimensional, and relentless. There was no one I could talk to. I grew isolated and self-conscious. My dyslexia made things worse. I called it "the curse." It added more stress to my life and made everything harder.

I'm still amazed I never turned to drugs or alcohol. Maybe I was just too scared. I'd seen what they could do to people and didn't want that life. I had enough trouble already.

I would talk to my biological father in my head. Why are things so difficult? I felt he had been robbed of life. I would have given up my life to bring him back.

From an early age, I was told you have to give to get. I gave, but what I really wanted was peace of mind; I never received it. Every child deserves to live without fear.

When it was finally time to go home, I felt a sense of relief. High school, though isolated, felt safe. I missed my stepsisters once they left. On my last night in Kotzebue, I tossed in my sleeping bag, unable to rest.

BOOM! A shot rang out. I ran to the window. A man was slumped on the porch stairs next door. A little boy stood beside him. I turned away and cried. Why is this my reality?

My stomach churned. I felt like I was dying inside. Even joys up here came with an edge. I couldn't believe a teenager like me could get an ulcer. But maybe this was what trauma looked like.

Even though I was raised Catholic, I rarely attended church then or even now, but I constantly prayed alone, pleading for my family, father, mother, brother, and myself. I just wanted peace. What I got was silence from above.

CHAPTER 8
Powers of Persuasion

*S*till glancing out of my left eye, I could see the fireman opening the door and trying to cut off the door hinges. As he cut the top hinge on the driver's side door, I could hear the noise of the grinding saw's gas engine and see sparks flashing off the metal hinge.

Oh! Cool! Now they can finally get me out of here.

He worked rapidly, trying to cut that door off as multi-colored lights flashed around us. It is amazing what you can see with peripheral vision. All of my senses seemed to come into play when I most needed them.

Taking one breath in and letting it out was still a battle I felt I was losing. Even though I never felt myself slipping away, fighting for air seemed more difficult. I could see him cut the first hinge off. Hurray! As the man moved away from the door, it started to drop toward the ground. The bottom hinge was still attached to the truck; the door created leverage on the front part of the truck. That's the kind of leverage I did not need. As the door started its descent toward the ground, the steering wheel pressed into me with a strong force, pressing deeper into my chest. My ribs and my lungs felt like they were going to explode. Breathing became even more difficult.

"I can't breathe. Get it off. Get it off," I cried out. "There's no way I can survive. No chance."

WINTER HAD ARRIVED along with my final year of high school. Now, as a seventeen-year-old kid, I was still frustrated and frightened out of my mind as I continued to deal with the haunting visions that relentlessly plagued me, coupled with some other deep-rooted personal issues that I could not solve. It was to be a very long winter, but I was excited to graduate that summer.

Winters are cold, even in Anchorage, but not as cold as in rural Alaska. The snow was falling, and it was dark outside. The weekend was approaching, and as usual, my friends and I wanted to visit the video arcade. In those days, home video games weren't as high-quality as the arcade games. It was good, clean fun, and I had wonderful friends.

Hey, I am not trying to say I was innocent. Believe me, I did my fair share of stirring up trouble, you know, kid stuff. Some boys wreak havoc at school. I caused my parents some grief with my childish and irresponsible actions. I am deeply and profoundly sorry for the things I have done that have caused concern. I have no excuses and take full responsibility for the problems I caused them.

The school bell rang, marking the start of the weekend. Students trudged through the snow to reach the school buses. *Ah! A seat, all right! I couldn't wait to get to the arcade room tonight.*

Sitting on the cold bus seat near the middle, I had a vivid flashback. The woman hacked up with the ulu with blood spurting out of her head, the old woman who shot at us, and the person who was shot next door were all bunched together in the front of the aisle next to the bus driver. It was as if they were as real as you and me. Not a ghostly image, but solid flesh. I could clearly hear the woman's moans and cries for help, see the blood spurting out of her head, feel the weight of my cousin jumping on me, and see the guy slumped over. I sat there and watched in horror as students came on the bus, walking through them, laughing playfully. I don't know how long that hallucination lasted, but it stayed for a short while longer after the bus driver drove away. This was the first time I was mad because I was sick and tired of seeing these images, knowing they were in my head and not real. And it pissed me off that there was no one I could talk to for help.

Finally, the anger subsided as the bus pulled up at our stop. The hard reality of walking in the dark and the cold sobered me up quickly. Even though it was dark, I could still see the beautiful snow-capped mountains, which helped calm my mind. Those mountains seemed to have a life of their own. Prominent and brilliant peaks projecting toward the endless sky. I loved seeing those mountains. They seemed timeless. They have been around for thousands, or possibly millions, of years. If they could talk, what would they say? I wish mountains and trees could speak. I would love to hear what they have to say. I would like to think they would tell us, "Take it easy, life is good. Forget about the bad things, enjoy what you have now." Looking at the mountains gave me a little peace of mind and a little hope. *One day, I will climb those mountains to see what's up there. I know I will find nothing, but climbing them will give me great satisfaction.*

That night, I went out with my girlfriend. She was a good soul, a kind and generous person. Though I didn't see much of her throughout the year, we got along well. I enjoyed her company and found her comforting. Her parents were very kind to me. They were a good, hardworking family. I have and continue to have a tremendous amount of respect for them.

Her brother and I used to banter back and forth when we were younger, as some boys do. I believe it was due to the competition because we were both in the same gym class. We would constantly see who could win the high jump. We eventually buried the hatchet and became friends. He was a great guy.

A week or so after we went out, she passed away. It was the last time I saw her. It broke my heart. I was devastated, missing her beautiful, infectious smile, her laugh, and her generosity. I felt so bad for her and her lovely family. She was a wonderful soul who was taken away from us early in life. *God bless her soul*, may she rest in peace. For some reason unknown to me, I was able to talk to my stepmom about this, and she was so gracious and compassionate, which gave me some relief while I was grieving for her. I think it was because she liked her.

Many people have friends that you don't see often. It might be months or even years before you see them again, but when you get together or talk to them long-distance, it is as if you have not missed one day without talking to them. You just pick up where you left off. What a warm, wonderful feeling. That's when you know you've been touched by something bigger than you. I was lucky to have some friends like that, like soulmates, whom I cherish to this day. I believe she and I had that special bond.

Even with that kind of relationship with my friends, I mostly kept my concerns about my future to myself. I had already realized that working in the bush was not for me. I just did not want to be around all that madness. I'd had enough of that and was still trying to cope with it. *What to do, what to do?* The question plagued me over and over again, like a broken record.

Months passed, winter was over, and school was coming to an end, leading to summer, a time of incredible beauty and great pain. I finally had a brief discussion with my stepfather about my future. I'll never forget it. It was a bright and sunny day. While standing in his living room looking out at the skyline, I saw Sleeping Lady, Mount McKinley, and other mountain ranges present themselves in all their glory. The great snow-peaked mountain ranges always took my breath away.

"You know, a person who knows how to dig holes will always have a job," he stated in a quiet but firm voice. "As opposed to a person who studies to dig holes, they may never have a job. I think you'll work in the bush using a shovel. Now you know you'll have a job."

"What about the military?" I asked. "I would like to join."

"Yes, the military is like a bunch of gears. If one of those gears breaks, then the whole thing comes to a stop."

"How about being a diesel mechanic or a plumber?" I softly asked.

"Diesel mechanics use big, heavy tools. No, I think you should be on the shovel."

I did not know why he was so adamant about my career. He must have thought I could handle the other trades because I'd had my pilot license for over two years. I was confused as to why he did the same thing to my brilliant and talented uncle, preventing him from realizing his dream job as an electrician, which was one of the reasons he came to Alaska in the first place. I felt so bad for him. It still pains me to this day.

I was unsure if he knew or understood what I'd gone through in the bush. Whenever I tried to bring it up, I was stopped in my tracks, and he again reminded me of how he dragged dead bodies from the lakes and rivers up onto the shore in some villages. "It's just life," he'd say.

Desperate and exhausted, plagued with the same old and new images in my head, I tried to reach out to other family members living out of state, including my beloved biological mother, who sadly passed away in 2024.

It turned out that she became a very successful fisherperson with her own commercial fishing boat, a child psychologist, a teacher, a pilot, and the first woman jet inspector for United Airlines.

While she was taking flying lessons, she fell in love with her marvelous flight instructor. A standup guy and one of the kindest people, you felt warm and safe being around. She was beautiful, and I miss her deeply. *God rest her soul.*

While talking to a relative about light general things, out of the blue, I was stunned when he said he had heard I was a sensitive child. All this without me even mentioning a word to anyone about what I had gone through. Not a peep. I know for a fact that none of my family members were aware of what I was going through. The only person who knew about it was my brother, but he learned of it about a decade after the fact. None of them had a clue about what I did and what had happened. I immediately kept silent and thought. *Yeah, well, none of you would ever have your children go out there. I guess it's OK for me to get shot at and witness horrible violence and all that, but not your kids. It would be a crime scene if your kid stubbed their toe at Disneyland.* I stewed with anger while keeping my mouth shut. It is safe to say I was a little upset.

I was just a kid. He must have known, for God's sake, he flew that hacked-up woman to Kotzebue. Didn't he see me? I helped him untie his 185 floatplane and push it off the shoreline as he powered up. Didn't he realize how something like that could adversely affect a child? Just sitting here writing about this pisses me off. I knew there was no hope of a discussion, so I gave up in the eighth grade. I was ashamed of telling him about the constant images and the struggles I endured, wreaking havoc in my life. Because of my inability to compartmentalize these horrible events, I showed weakness and childish behavior that put additional misunderstanding and strain on the family members in my inner circle, which caused me to be ashamed of myself at times.

I was not immune to his hypnotic powers of persuasion. He was ever so convincing that when you left his presence, you'd ask yourself, *What the hell just happened? What did I commit to?* I mean, I admired and respected him, but it was difficult, if not impossible, to say no to him. What was I to do? For crying out loud, he was one of the biggest Native contractors in the state. So where was I to go?

Since I'd first met him, he'd been kind and gentle to me, and I never sensed that he had a mean bone in his body. Even though we hardly talked,

I always sensed that he was sympathetic to the circumstances of how I became his adopted son. He was gifted with high intelligence; like his father, my grandfather, he was an avid reader with a wide range of knowledge and skill sets. As he grew older, I observed him refining his business and persuasion skills to achieve his goals. I am pretty sure he was a genius, just like his brother.

As I left the house in a daze, I looked at the magnificent mountain ranges. The bright sky turned dark; the mountains started to dim. Anger ran up and down my spine. *How could this be? Why do I have to go?* How come things can be so good but so bad at the same time? I should be celebrating graduating, but what was there to celebrate? The only thing I could think of was that he was trying to teach me a lesson about some of the silly things I had done. I really did not have a clue what his motives were. All I could think about was the future, and I didn't know how much time I had left on earth, knowing the inherent risk of working out in the bush. At age eighteen, I felt my freedom of choice was stripped away from me, and my future was lost forever.

I was always told that I had it made. "You don't have to pay for transportation, food, or lodging. You work a lot of overtime, and there is no place to spend your money." Yes, you can make a lot of money, but consider how other industries' employers compensate workers. Is it worth it for the average worker based in town to leave their loved ones, friends, and home behind for many months without going home for breaks? Housing, clothes, cars, insurance, and other costs continue. The average worker has to pay those running costs they can't use while working hard in the field. Then, when you get back to town, you still have to spend the hard-earned money you have made to live on because you are now unemployed and have no income. So, what do you have? There are no medical or retirement benefits, just unemployment.

Many workers tended to run out of money quickly, so many tried to get another job. Usually, the jobs are finished by mid-winter. As trade workers know, it can be difficult to find work during that time because contractors typically don't start to hire until late in the spring or summer after the snow and frozen ground melt. The running joke from many of my colleagues was that, when it spread out throughout the year, our pay was not much better than working at McDonald's.

In contrast, depending on their position, state workers based in town who worked in the bush typically spent short periods in the field. Many of them worked for a few days or a couple of weeks, but no more than a month at a time. When they returned, they still retained their job and continued to receive pay throughout the year, which included medical and pension benefits. Many North Slope oil employees working in Prudhoe Bay worked two weeks on and two weeks off, and continued to receive pay while they were off.

While comparing various workforce compensation does not diminish anyone's trade, hard work, risk, and sacrifice in the field, it does highlight how different industries' employers compensate their workers.

After my discussion with my stepdad, I knew my life would change. Things would be challenging, and I had to get hard fast. Little did I know at that time just how challenging my life would become. Nothing in my past or present could have fully prepared me for the chain of events that would follow me for the rest of my life.

CHAPTER 9
Pitkas Point

A look of horror came over his face as he realized that the driver's-side door had slipped down and the steering wheel was crushing me even more. He sprinted over even though he was only about two or three steps away, grabbed the bottom of the door, and pushed it back up to relieve the pressure from the steering wheel.

Wow! What a relief! Oh, man!

Feeling that steering wheel inch forward was a shock. While I was still struggling to breathe, another fireman came around, grabbed the grinding saw, and cut the lower hinge off. Then, boom! Off came the door. Freedom was at hand. I wondered how they were going to slide me out of the truck since my legs, feet, and chest were still pinned.

I had my answer soon enough. A man came toward the open door with a strange piece of equipment. I recognized that tool, which my uncle, a volunteer firefighter, had told me about. I had always wanted to see the Jaws of Life in action, widening constricted openings, but I most certainly did not want to see this great tool working to extract me from a vehicle.

I could hear the roar of the little engine coming from the Jaws of Life. The man took the tool and placed the tip of it in the lower part of the driver's side. Then, the two long metal arms started to spread apart.

Oh, here we go. I will be a free man.

As he spread the lower part to create a bigger hole, my feet and legs began to get crushed. Newton's theory was correct; for every action, there is an equal and opposite reaction. This theory was now being proved true in the most painful way.

He continued to widen the hole, and my legs began to hurt more and more. Thank God the pressure on my chest didn't increase.

"Hey, hey, you're going the wrong way!" I yelled.

The man stopped immediately, quickly removed the Jaws of Life and moved it to a different area. Then, the opening slowly widened until I could move my legs around. Oh! What a feeling! I was almost free. I could barely breathe since the steering wheel was still trapping me, but I could move my legs, and I knew I would not die in that truck. If I were going to die, then at least I would be out of that twisted metal.

AFTER GRADUATING FROM HIGH SCHOOL, life underwent rapid changes. I could hang out with friends I'd always enjoyed, so life was good. I tried my best to forget the bush. I wanted to keep that deep in my mind while dealing with the flashbacks.

Oh, the hot, sunny summer days in Alaska; how exquisite they truly are. This was turning out to be a splendid summer for everybody. I had just signed on as a carpenter's apprentice with my stepfather's subcontractor, Brian, whom I had known from the first time I went to Kiana. He was a young man in his early twenties who was either a self-made millionaire or was knocking on the back door to it.

He had been working for my father, both directly and indirectly, since the age of fifteen. At that age, he'd dropped out of high school and lived independently. I think he eventually obtained his GED. Brian was a handsome, short, stocky man with solid muscles and curly red hair. He was brilliant and had no shortage of girlfriends.

He had a positive aura, always laughing and smiling, and people wanted to be around him everywhere he went. I have always liked and respected him. He was one of the hardest and most driven man I'd had ever met. Even though he was a workaholic, he knew how to play hard, much like my stepfather. He gave my stepfather a run for his money when it came to putting in the hours for work. Regardless of his success, I still wanted to be a diesel mechanic or plumber. Oh well, I guess learning how to build houses was OK.

Brian told me we were going to build a new school addition at Pitkas Point, but first, we were going to frame up his new home, which was about a forty-minute drive north of Anchorage. I have seen his company's ups and downs throughout the years and marveled at his ability to make a comeback and keep moving forward. His ability to avoid financial ruin when most would have given up was remarkable. He always said he would rather have the problem job than no job. And I think that philosophy permitted him never to quit.

The story of his accomplishments in his private life and business at such a young age is mind-boggling. Whatever he touched turned to gold; he oozed success. Nobody, and I do mean nobody, could tell him what to do. Not ever. And now I was going to help him frame up his house on a piece of land that had a private airstrip so he could park his favorite plane at his home.

He and his lead carpenter and friend, Tim, whom I also knew from my days in Kiana and Kotzebue, frequently yelled at each other while building his house. They were similar in age, and it seemed that was how they usually talked to each other and the crew. At that time, Brian would yell at me, but Tim never yelled at me or the other crew members. They both pushed the job forward harder and harder to accomplish their goals.

Come to think about it, I don't think they knew they were yelling. What I do know is that the projects they worked on in the bush were, at times, extremely stressful. As a very young boss, he had tremendous responsibility for fulfilling contractual agreements, payroll, and keeping work crews happy. Though it bothered me, I never faulted them for yelling at each other. It's how it was in those days.

In contrast, my stepfather. I never heard him yell or get emotional, no matter how much stress he endured. I had been working on his jobs since I was eight years old. Heck, I was even the elevator boy for his grand openings. I had never been yelled at while working on his jobs or at home, so it was a little strange for me to be yelled at while working for someone else. As exhausting as being yelled at was, believe me, it was a lot easier to deal with than being exposed to horrific acts of violence on any day of the week.

Shortly after we erected his house, he flew me to St. Mary's-Pitkas Point Airport in his private plane. He told me we would be staying at the Roadhouse near the local airport. St. Mary's population is around 600 people, located some 440 air miles west of Anchorage on the Andreafski River. The Andreafski River flows south to the Yukon River. Pitkas Point, which has a population of around 185 people, is located approximately five miles upstream from where Andreafski merges into the Yukon River, and about three miles from the airport.

As we flew out to St. Mary's in his Pacer taildragger, it was the first time I had ever flown with him in that type of plane. He loved that plane, and with good reason. He said it was like flying a kite, and it did feel that way in the air. The land was flat for miles as we approached our destination. The terrain was much different than Anchorage. It was somewhat similar to the Arctic, but not. It looked swampy, with little lakes everywhere.

Finally, after hours of flying, I saw the great Yukon River for the first time. Wow! It was so wide, it was huge. *There should be a lot of fish in there. No sheefish, though. Those are usually found in the Arctic.*

After landing at the airport, we went to our camp. The Roadhouse camp was clean, warm, and reasonably comfortable. Plus, we could get food anytime because it also had a mini diner. Showers were also available, along with laundry facilities and clean sheets.

We were scheduled to work at Pitkas Point for two or three weeks before returning home for the Fourth of July. I think he had a date. I was excited and nervous about my new job and didn't want to disappoint my new boss or stepdad. I was of legal age now, so I felt I had to start acting like a grown-up and make amends to my parents for my shameful misdeeds while attending high school.

Our first job at Pitkas Point was to lay out the foundation. Although I had worked on many different types of foundations, after a few minutes of discussion, it became clear that this foundation was much different and more complicated than the ones we'd used up north.

You see, there are many pockets of permafrost throughout Alaska. Our job was to dig holes in the frozen ground, approximately sixteen to twenty feet deep, so that the long, thick steel pilings could be placed into the holes and protrude about four feet above ground. Once set, we backfilled the gap in the holes with the melted mud slurry and then refrigerated the pilings until they froze, which, in theory, should freeze back the mud slurry that typically stayed frozen all year. If the ground does not melt, the building should not sink. It is a sound system, but it is just expensive.

As soon as we got to the job site, it was as if his muscle memory of yelling went into high gear all day long. It was, "Get this, get that, do this, do that!" I ran whenever he needed something to be done; I never walked. He pushed me to the max. I kept thinking how lucky I was to be in good shape. Holy cow! I was worn out, and we hadn't even had lunch yet. I just kept my mouth shut and did what I was told.

All the yelling and running can't last too much longer. Maybe if I work hard and show him I'm not a bum, he will lighten up a little. Brian knew I was a hard worker, so I didn't understand why he felt it necessary to push me so hard. I suppose this was what it was like on a framing crew.

For lunch, I usually have a couple of sandwiches. It's amazing how everything tastes good when you're hungry. They were probably nothing more than tuna or peanut butter sandwiches, but it seemed like the finest chef had made them.

A few days later, two drillers, pilings, and a drill rig arrived. That night, the older driller told us how difficult drilling through permafrost can be. He cautioned us not to get shaken up if we didn't reach our goal of four holes a day. The leader was an older, funny man who was full of life and reminded me of Grandpa. These guys, both wild and nice, had worked for the oil companies drilling holes in the Arctic. I am sure they had seen a lot throughout their years.

The next morning, the two drillers set up their drill rig, a truck equipped with a motor and augers. These augers were four feet in length and about sixteen inches wide. The older driller stood near the mark for the first post, guiding the truck toward the mark. After he lined up the truck, they were ready to install the first auger. This was exciting stuff for me.

The younger driller went over to the side of the truck and pulled out the first of many four-foot-long augers. He placed it into the hook and hung the auger in place. Then, the elderly man jumped back on the truck and took control of the drill bit's levers. He could adjust the rotation speed and move the auger up, down, side to side, or forward and backward. He carefully maneuvered the auger down toward the ground, making slight adjustments until he struck the previously surveyed mark. The auger plunged into the soil. Then, the younger driller took his level out and adjusted the auger until it was plumb. The rotation began, and the auger spun downward. Every few minutes, we had to remove the excess dirt and mud from the hole, being careful not to get the shovel caught in the spinning auger. The driller would randomly check the auger for plumb. After placing the next auger on the drill, he checked again and found it slightly out of plumb.

"It goes where it wants to," he said. "Nothing we can do about it."

These augers were cutting through the soil like butter. I kept thinking, *This is easy, no problem. We'll be out of here soon.* We installed the third auger and were now down about eight feet or so. Suddenly, without warning, the drilling came almost to a dead stop. The auger was spinning, but nothing was happening. It just kept spinning.

The ground became stubborn. We had a permafrost hit. Well, that shattered my presumption of getting back to town sooner.

Finally, we began making a little progress again, and I found out what the older driller meant when he'd talked about "mud balls." As the auger turned, it brought up frozen balls of mud about two and a half inches around; they looked like chocolate balls. It was cool and made me hungry for donuts.

Once, we reached the depth we needed. We pulled out the augers one at a time until they were clear of the deep hole we had just made. Now the first piling was ready to be installed. The operator moved the drill rig to the heavy pilings. We hooked a strap to his drill rig and wrapped it around the long, heavy piling. He lifted it into the air and put it straight down into the middle of the hole. We had to ensure the pipes were level before backfilling them with the melted mud tailings slurry, which required the use of a stinger to vibrate the mud back around the pipes, similar to what is used for concrete.

Vibrating removes air pockets and distributes the mud throughout the spacing between the pipe and the wall of the hole; *one down and many to go.*

Throughout the day, the weather went from hot and sunny to cold, windy, and rainy. We would stay and work ten to twelve hours daily, regardless of the weather. In those days, non-union companies didn't have any breaks—at least, I never got one. You just worked, and that was it.

That didn't bother me too much then, but I kept wondering whether this was how it would be for the rest of my career.

We completed our job on time and returned to Anchorage just in time for the Fourth of July celebration. Home. Back home. A place where I could rest for just a short while and not have to be yelled at all day. That would be a relief. Man, I was tired after working at a dead run. I felt as if I was training for a marathon. I was worn out from head to toe. Every inch of my body wanted to rest.

After a few days off in town, I was able to reflect on the job we had done. Oh! What a good feeling! We'd accomplished so much in a short amount of time. I was proud and excited. I remember going upstairs and seeing Brian standing next to the big window. Outside, the sky was so blue, and the mountain range was magnificent. Mount McKinley was in full view. I never grew tired of looking at the mountains. He reached over, shook my hand, handed me my first pay envelope, and said, "Now you know why we do this." I looked him in the eye and thanked him.

When I opened the envelope, I saw a big number. My heart was pounding. *Wow! That's a lot of money.* I was either lucky or unlucky, depending on how you look at it. Pitkas Point was a high-paying, Davis-Bacon state job. There are high-, medium-, and low-paying Davis-Bacon jobs. The lower paying jobs we called mini-bacon. Unfortunately, the mini-bacon wage was so low that it was difficult to make a living on it.

Before long, the Fourth of July was upon us, one of my favorite times of the year. My friends and I got good seating, and the weather was hot and clear. I had fun with my friends, blasting fireworks and listening to music. I tried to forget my problems for a brief moment. I thought about my sweet girlfriend, who couldn't be there. *Godspeed to you, angel.* They don't call the state the land of the midnight sun for nothing, because even during the fireworks show in Anchorage, it was still somewhat light outside.

After the Fourth, it was time to return to Pitkas Point. After a couple of sleepless nights trying to figure out how to deal with all the yelling, I decided to tough it out because the Roadhouse was clean, and the food was good. For the first time, I believed that I would not be around any violence, and I felt relatively safe. We finally boarded a plane, and off we went to Pitkas Point. When we arrived, things were a little bit different. There were a few more men on the job some of whom I knew from the Kiana and Kotzebue days, some I'd never met. The Roadhouse was about a fifteen-minute drive from the Pitkas Point job site and about halfway to St. Mary's. A dusty gravel road connected the two villages.

We were lucky that the weather was hot. It was very nice outside, just the kind of thing I needed to keep my spirits up. I even had my own room at the Roadhouse, and that suited me just fine, especially since I had brought a cassette tape player and some silly tapes. High school stuff. It was a little piece of home, something to hang on to. I was hoping I would not lose my mind out there.

Even though I recognized all the things we were accomplishing for the good of society, I saw no future for myself. *What kind of life was this? Being away from your family and friends to make a living? Why not just work where you want to live?* Those questions continued to haunt me. Why was I complaining? Deep inside my heart and mind, I knew the answer: self-identification. I was young and wanted to be my own person and create things in life.

At times, life can be a little boring out in the bush. If you don't have access to a boat, airplane, or outdoor activity, there is nothing to do. So, how do you pass the time while waiting for materials to arrive? Good question. Sure, it's easy to sit there and come up with creative ideas, but when there is no access to materials, it can drive a person crazy just waiting to get to work. Sometimes we would wait for days. You can't simply jump on a plane to go home and then return immediately, because commercial flights may not be available. It would be on us to pay for the round trip, and we would not receive payment for those days off, which at the end of the year made a significant difference in our actual wages earned.

A few days later, the barge arrived with the materials on the great Yukon River. First, we started installing the foundation beams on the frozen pilings. Working around the other guys was cool; they were nice to me, and I liked them. None of them yelled at me, not even Tim. I know Brian liked them all as well. Still, I was worn out from his yelling all day. I was also physically tired from running and work; it felt like I was training for a marathon. Every morning, I would have to mentally psych myself up, like taking deep breaths before going underwater. I knew I would be in a lot of pain that day, both mentally and physically, so I needed to try to prepare myself. Even on the one day a week when we rested, we fought boredom and isolation.

After we assembled the floor system, I helped build my first thick wall, which was approximately twenty feet tall. This wall, in particular, was hefty. It was built using two-by-tens, which included blocking and half-inch plywood sheathing. As it lay on the deck fully assembled, I wondered how it was possible to lift something so massive. Both Brian and Tim yelled at each other, trying to resolve this problem. I was starting to giggle. It was like watching a comedy team.

Years later, while talking to Tim with a small group of people, for some unknown reason, I mentioned the pale woman with the blood spurting out of her head in Kiana and that I'd gotten her help. Tim stared at me with rage, and his face turned beet red. His eyes pierced through me as he snapped back at me with a strong, bitter voice, saying it was he who had helped that lady. I asked, "What are you talking about? I ran around trying to get help." Again, he angrily barked back, "I saved her." This sent chills up my spine because I had no memory of seeing him during that incident. I felt bad for him because it was obvious that I had unknowingly triggered an event that had traumatized him.

A strange thing occurred to me. Since I had never discussed what I had witnessed with anyone, I felt slightly relieved, as if ten pounds had lifted off my back. The flashback of her seemed less vivid, but the other images remained with the same intensity, and perhaps even more so. I kept thinking about Tim and wondered if maybe he was one of the people who had helped bandage her bloody head, which may have sprayed blood all over his body and soaked into his clothing. I mean, when I saw her being placed on my stepfather's airplane, the rags wrapped around her head were dripping wet with blood.

They contemplated lifting the wall by hand or with manual pump jacks. Either way, we had to prepare the wall for lifting. The problem was that the floor system cantilevered six feet past the pilings, and on top of that, the floor beams were not securely attached to the pilings. Since the wall was so heavy, they worried that erecting it could lift the rear floor system off the pilings, causing it to slide downward toward the ground and send the wall back toward us, smashing down on the floor and crashing thousands of pounds of material onto us, squashing us like bugs. So, yeah, I was a bit nervous.

They wanted to try lifting the wall by hand that day, so Brian rounded up about ten men from somewhere in town to help our crew. Since the wall was already prepared, everyone lined up along the top of the wall to lift. "OK, everybody, lift! Lift!" Brian exclaimed.

We all bent over and started to lift. Every muscle in my body was straining, and I could hear the other men grunting as they strained to lift the wall just to knee height. Brian yelled, "Set it back down." What a heavy wall, holy cow! A failed attempt.

Now, we knew wall jacks were the only way to lift the wall. Preparing the wall jacks only took about twenty minutes. Once done, we returned to camp and waited a couple of days for the floor jacks and additional extended ladders to arrive.

We were ready to lift the wall once they arrived. A pump jack works similarly to a car jack, except it cranks up a double two-by-four. I think we had about four to five jacks for the entire length of the top of the wall. People either volunteered or were picked to operate the manual levers. I was picked. I did not volunteer because I had never seen or done anything like that before and did not know what to expect. Each person operating the jacks had a step ladder and an extension ladder nearby.

The trick to raising the wall was that the operators had to be in sync while lifting it. Brian directed us to the top. Standing on the floor, we raised the wall until we could no longer reach the lever. Then, we stood on step ladders and continued pumping the wall, which was now directly over our heads, up until we could not reach the lever again. *Oh, great!* I thought. *Now I have two things to worry about. Having the wall fall back down and crush us, and having enough nerve to climb twenty feet in the air to finish raising the wall.*

Once we had the extended ladders leaning on the top plate of the wall, the ladders were freed up to slide on the top plate while we continued to climb and pump the wall up plumb. *Oh man,* I thought. *This sucker is getting high.* Climbing up that ladder was exciting, but also frightening. I admit it made me more nervous than I would have thought.

We still had a long way to go before we could fully erect the wall. Each of us started pumping at the same time. As we approached the top, without warning, the wall lunged forward a couple of feet. Wow, that startled me. My body was shaking, as I was about eighteen feet in the air. I wanted to continue, but I couldn't stop shaking. Recognizing my inexperience and growing anxiety, my boss told me to come down from the ladder and help brace the wall after it was fully erected.

Cool, I thought.

Even though he yelled most of the day, it felt good knowing he recognized that I was trying and willing to finish the job, and that he cared for my safety and that of others. So, he took over, climbed the ladder, and completed the job.

Finally, the wall was up and braced, and the floor hadn't collapsed under us. Everything had turned out OK, no problem, and no big deal. I just stood back and looked at that massive wall we'd built. The crew was so nice. Nobody criticized me for climbing down. I think they were all happy that nobody got hurt. The day wore on as we continued to work toward evening, and then we went to the Roadhouse for a good meal and rest.

I kept thinking about that wall and what an accomplishment it was. It was really a sight to see, and if we were working back in town, a wall like that would typically be raised using a crane to make it easier and safer for the crews. There was a lot of pride that day. I felt as if we had done something pretty neat.

Weeks went by, and we finally got to the roof. After working day in and day out with only short lunch breaks, we were finally getting close to the end of the job. My body was sore, aching, and worn out from the long, hard days. I couldn't wait to get back to Anchorage. I missed my friends and home and was ready for a well-deserved rest.

Although I was getting good experience, I wanted a short break. I had heard a rumor about a big job coming up, and I wasn't sure if my stepfather had gotten the bid. I was always proud whenever my stepdad got a new job. The amount of effort and energy he invested in the bidding process required a significant amount of work. Obtaining financing, bonding, and determining the most effective way to transport the material to the job site required considerable imagination and forethought. Logistics, where to place the material and crew housing, was probably the most challenging part of the job. Damn, I hoped he would get that job soon, so we would not have to work in the winter. At least right now, the weather felt good: hot and sunny during the day, but clear and cold at night.

The job with Brian had taught me a lot, and those lessons continued with learning how to install a screwless metal roof. Brian was hooked up on the high roof with a harness belt while I was on the ground. He and the lead carpenter were screwing metal clips onto the steep roof while shouting down to me, instructing me on how these metal roofs go together. The most important point was to make sure the metal sheets ran square to the framed-in roof.

My job was to carefully slide the long metal sheets close enough to the building to clip on a pair of vise C-clamps on the top metal end, then attach the dangling ropes from the roof. As they pull the metal up, I would help guide the metal sheet until I could no longer reach it. He had so much knowledge and experience with roofs that my head was spinning at how fast they laid that metal down. They completed the laying of the main sheets in under a day. It took about half a day to finish the trim. It looked beautiful.

A few days later, Brian took off and left Pitkas Point. Most of the crew, including a couple of plumbers, stayed and continued to work. I liked the lead plumber. I met him in Anchorage, and he was Brian's roommate. He made me smile and laugh all the time. I mean, his nickname was Yukon Horn. Now that's funny. The other plumber was a character, too, a bearded wild man who looked like a biker, and he loved his booze and drugs. I'll never forget the first time I met him. Without saying hello, he'd asked strangers with a straight face, "You got any booze, any drugs?" That was it. You knew where you stood with him. Whenever my uncle and I saw him, we usually laughed because he would ask the same question every time.

Brian had brought his truck to the job site, a white Chevy truck with four big balloon tires and a roll bar. It was a nice truck, and he had a lot of fun driving it.

However, the large tires made it tricky to maneuver because it was prone to sliding around on the loose gravel. Unfortunately, I would find out the hard way just how squirrely it was to drive.

CHAPTER 10

Decisions

*F*inally, I could slightly wiggle about the cab. Maybe I moved two or three inches, and even though the steering wheel's pressure was off my chest, it was still painful to breathe. I was fighting for my life.

A man reached in around me. Grabbing me by my shoulders, he pulled me out of that chewed-up metal and immediately placed me on a gurney. Oh, yes! I was lying down flat. I was in a lot of pain, but what a relief to get out of that truck after two and a half hours or perhaps longer.

The temperature was still around freezing. I saw somebody putting a blanket on me and I felt a little more secure even though I still wasn't sure I was going to survive this ordeal.

Boom, boom, clank, clank, up into the ambulance I went.

"You'll be OK!" somebody called out. "It's going to take a while for us to get to the hospital, maybe half an hour or so, but first, we need to take you to the nearest trauma center."

"Just make sure you drive slowly; the roads are icy," I said. The back doors slammed shut, and the ambulance started its long drive to the trauma center.

A FEW DAYS after Brian left, I wanted to get out for a little while, away from the Roadhouse, to look at the moon and the sky and to see St. Mary's. I got the keys to the truck, jumped in, and took off. I wasn't planning to be gone for very long, maybe just half an hour. Little did I know how tired I really was.

The road to St. Mary's was fairly straight. I don't remember many turns. It was dark and cold, with a temperature of around 28 degrees Fahrenheit. I was admiring the moon and the stars. They were out in their full glory. *Man! They were so clear and bright out in the bush, with no city lights spoiling the view of the stars.* Glancing in the rear-view mirror, I saw dust flying high thanks to the big balloon tires.

Driving down the gravel road, I thought about my job and friends while trying to unwind from the day. Then I recognized I was exhausted.

My hands hurt, and my legs burned from running around that day.

What is next? I wondered. *What is the next job?*

I noticed the tundra on both sides of me. My arms were tired, and my head slowly dipped down, then up. The roar of the engine faded away. I was completely unaware of how fast I was going, but I didn't look at the speedometer because I figured I was driving at a safe speed. After all, I didn't want to wreck Brian's truck. I just wanted to unwind from the day.

A short while later, I looked down at the speedometer and casually noticed that I was going too fast: seventy miles an hour. Everything seemed to be happening in slow motion. I must have fallen asleep at the wheel. As I looked directly in front of me, I could see the road, but it was moving in slow motion. The truck felt like it was sliding to the right.

Oh, I thought, *I'm going into the ditch*.

My reactions were slow. It was as though time was standing still. I wasn't upset or scared.

Hey, I better get back on the road, I told myself.

Just saying the words in my head felt like an eternity. As I started to turn the wheel to the left, I could feel the vehicle's rear end lose its grip on the gravel shoulder.

Wow, I am sliding, I thought.

Suddenly, the truck swerved back and forth, and I was completely out of control. It felt like minutes were passing while I tried to make course corrections, even though everything was taking place in fractions of a second.

The truck started rotating clockwise while my body pressed hard on the driver's side door. Up and up, my body rose as I sat inside the truck.

As I looked straight out through the front windshield with the headlights on high, I could see the truck starting to roll over. I remember seeing both the right and left windshield wiper blades sticking out.

I am going to crash, I thought.

I continued to feel weirdly calm. I was not frightened or worried. I didn't see my life flash before my eyes or anything like that, but I did wonder what kind of chance I had rolling a pickup truck out in the middle of nowhere.

No chance.

Without explanation, I did not wear my seatbelt. I was baffled as to why this was, because we all wore seatbelts during the winter because of the snowy and icy conditions. I was also a trained pilot, and it was mandatory to wear safety belts. Despite taking risks and seeming a bit wild as a child and young adult, I had been raised with safety in mind.

The truck kept rolling and rolling.

I guess I'm going to die. A clear thought hit me slowly.

I could still hear the roar of the engine and the tires grinding into the gravel road. I could feel the pressure on my body as the truck rolled. I saw the tundra on both sides of me, even as the truck rose and turned. I was upside down. The windshield wiper blades came into view, and then the road. It looked close, too close. The gravel felt like it was right in front of my face. It seemed like I could count the rocks. That's how slow everything felt.

Still looking forward, I watched the front of the truck slam into the road. The cab hit the ground faster than the blink of an eye. I heard metal crunching close by. Then I realized I was outside the rolling truck, my body scraping along the gravel. I have no memory of being ejected.

Sliding on my back, getting torn up, I saw the truck's headlights flashing as it spun, round and round. The crunch of metal grew fainter in the distance. Then, suddenly, a hard thump. I came to a complete stop.

Lying flat on my back, my eyes opened. I could see my breath in the cold night. Oh, the pain. I blinked slowly, again and again.

Am I alive or dead? I wondered. I'd never died before, so I had no idea what to expect. Do we still feel pain, physical or emotional, after death? Are our thoughts whole, or just fragments? Do we carry those thoughts with us somehow, right up until we're buried? And if I was dead, why hadn't I seen the light? People often talk about the tunnel when describing their near-death stories.

I was confused. Still lying on my back, blinking, I heard the truck engine roaring in the distance. Off to the side, I saw a bright light. I assumed it was the headlights of the truck I had just rolled.

It was cold, bitterly cold. I had no idea how long I'd been lying there for seconds, minutes, maybe hours. My back throbbed from the lumpy, frozen tundra beneath me. I hadn't turned my head or moved my arms, which were stretched out above me like I was being held at gunpoint.

I kept breathing, in and out, trying to stay calm. What now? What to do and how? First, I needed to know if my feet and legs still worked.

I couldn't move. I tried, but nothing worked, not even my feet, toes, hands, arms, fingers, or my head. Nothing. Only my eyelids were blinking.

Am I paralyzed? I wondered. *Oh, God. What should I do?*

"Help me," I said calmly. *I've got to see if my feet work. I have to know.*

I lay there, engulfed in pain. I didn't budge. I seemed paralyzed, if not physically, then in my mind.

Dear God, what's happened? Dad, help me, please! What do I do?

Strangely, I still wasn't afraid. I cried out for help because it seemed like the thing to do, but there was no one there. I had to decide whether to try to move or stay lying on the tundra. My body wouldn't cooperate. Somehow, I had to find the strength.

I focused on my toes. I rolled my eyes toward my feet and, miraculously, felt a flicker of movement. My chest heaved; my heart pounded. But then my toes went still, and my eyes drifted back toward the night sky. That tiny effort drained me. I needed to rest before trying again.

The truck engine still roared. I saw bright lights off to the side, which I assumed were headlights. It was bitterly cold. I didn't know how long I'd been lying there. Seconds? Minutes? Hours? Pain radiated through my back. I hadn't moved my head or arms, which were stretched out above me like I was being held at gunpoint. I breathed slowly, trying to stay calm.

What now? What to do, and how?

First, I had to know if my legs still worked.

I could feel my heart beating faster. My chest rose and fell. I was barely able to move my feet. Up and down, just a few times. Then I rested again. My limbs were still unresponsive, the pain agonizing.

Am I alive or dead? I asked myself again. *If I'm dead, this sure hurts.*

Minutes passed. I focused on trying to move my legs. My toes twitched, then my feet rotated. My breathing quickened. My legs didn't respond, but I knew I wasn't paralyzed. I couldn't move my arms or hands yet; they remained stretched above me. Still, if I could wiggle my toes, there was hope.

Exhausted again, I rested.

Oh, God, what am I supposed to do? I thought. *I have to get out of here.*

Then, movement. My hands began to shift. Pain pulsed through me. My right hand flopped onto my chest, then my left to my stomach. I hadn't meant to move them; they just moved. My heart pounded. I was spent. But now I could turn my head slowly, side to side.

I have to get out of here.

Time to try getting up. I closed my eyes briefly, then opened them and pulled my knees slowly toward my chest. It felt like an entertaining. I let them fall back to the ground.

I thought of people with spinal cord injuries, fine one moment, paralyzed the next, because someone moved them too soon. That could be me.

What now? What should I do?

My thoughts wandered. Strange how your mind drifts in moments like that. I saw the stars above, sharp in the cold sky. I lifted my left hand and stared. Blood dripped from it.

How bad am I? I wondered. *Sh*t, I must be dead or seriously hurt.*

One more try, I thought. *I need to get out of here.*

The engine still roared. I worried the truck might explode. I closed my eyes again, heart thudding. Then, with effort, my knees rose toward my chest. My hands slid from my chest to the ground. I grunted, moaned, and struggled. Rolling onto my side, I pressed my hands into the frozen tundra and got to my feet.

The truck's headlights glowed in the distance. My stomach burned with pain.

This is bad. Should I turn the engine off?

Despite everything, I tried to assess my situation. My right sock and shoe were gone. I was barefoot. My pants were torn, my shirt shredded, blood dripping from my head to my toes.

Am I alive or dead? I still asked myself. *If I'm dead, what a mess. What a bloody disaster. Is this what I'd look like heading to heaven or hell? Not exactly dressed to meet my Maker. But if I'm alive, I'm in deep trouble.*

I turned and looked at the gravel road. It seemed so far away.

How will I make it to the road, let alone the Roadhouse? I have to get back. I need help.

Surprisingly, I remained calm. Each breath fogged the air in front of me. Blood was everywhere. I took a step—pain shot through the bottom of my right foot. I eased up, then stepped again. The brushy, frozen tundra crunched beneath me like an icy sponge. Twigs and leaves stabbed my bare foot. I limped toward the dirt road. My foot burned.

Eventually, I reached the edge. I stood there, catching my breath. Blood still dripped freely. I turned side to side.

Which way was the camp? I hesitated. *OK. If I walk toward the truck, then that must be the way I came. I can turn off the engine and head back.*

Still standing on the tundra, I wasn't sure I had the strength. I felt faint. If I wasn't dead yet, I was close. But I had to try. I took a deep breath and stepped onto the gravel. My foot screamed in pain.

I limped toward the truck, babying my bare foot. Blood dripped from my head and hands. I looked up. The stars were bright. Even now, I saw beauty as I staggered toward the wreckage.

Thoughts of my past rushed in. Bush life. The bleeding woman whose husband had cut her blood spurting from her head. The old woman firing a gun, my cousin shielding me with his body.

I tried to shake the visions, but they wouldn't stop. They plagued me as I fought to survive.

Please, God, stop them! I screamed silently. *Stop the pictures. Help me. Please, help me.*

I was in shock. That had to be it. Still, I made a slow, straight, steady track toward the truck. My body hurt, especially in my stomach.

People say your life flashes before your eyes when you're about to die. That didn't happen to me. All I saw were those f**king visions.

I tried to shut them out. I thought of my father, Gordon. I missed him so much. Was I about to see him? I fought like hell to stay alive and begged for his help. I didn't want to die out here alone.

Father, please don't let me die out here. Please help me.

Finally, I reached the truck. It was upright and still running. The headlights were so bright they made me squint and turn away. The truck looked like a crushed-up aluminum can, but the engine sounded smooth. I didn't want to get too close. Maybe the gas tank was leaking. I didn't want to stick around and find out.

I touched the driver's side door and it was cold. I tried to pull my hand back, but I couldn't move. A moment later, I ducked my head through the shattered window of the caved-in cab and reached for the key. It was a long stretch, but I finally turned it. The engine stopped.

The headlights stayed on. I stared at them, wondering if I should turn them off. Why the hell was I even thinking about the lights?

How in the hell did I survive this wreck? Or did I survive?

In reflection, the answer was obvious; leaving the lights on made more sense. I needed help. I was bleeding all over, so why was I thinking about headlights?

OK then, damn it, I'll just leave them on.

Yeah, that's it. I'll leave them on so that if someone drives by, they'll see and maybe stop.

As I pushed myself out of the window, I wondered if I'd cut myself on any glass or metal. I couldn't feel anything. Maybe that was good. Just another thing to worry about later. Right now, I had to get help. Time was running out.

I paused. Looked up. The stars were stunning, and the moon lit up the pitch-black night.

OK. Which way? Right or left?

If I head, the wrong way toward St. Mary's, I might die.

Damn. What am I going to do?

Even if I tried for the Roadhouse, there was no guarantee I'd make it. And if I stayed here, maybe someone would find me. I made my decision. I started walking toward the Roadhouse.

Come on, Dave. You can make it.

CHAPTER 11

Coin Flip

I Could, hear the ambulance sirens as we started to drive away from that twisted metal. I was strapped on a gurney with medical equipment hooked up to me. My ribs were hurting. The pain was everywhere. There seemed to be nothing I could do about the pain. I never once thought about needing painkillers. I can't explain why. Maybe I was in shock.

I was extremely lucky and, at the same time, unlucky. I could see and hear the paramedics, but I wasn't sure what they were working on. One thing I did know for sure is that I was cold, real cold.

The road was bumpy, and I bounced around. Knowing the road was still icy, I felt a little nervous. I just didn't want to get into another accident. I could feel us slide around a little. I had every confidence in the driver and paramedics; it was the other cars I was concerned about.

"We are taking you to Royal Inland Hospital in Kamloops," one of the paramedics shouted to me over the road noise and sirens. "But first we have to take you to a trauma center."

He seemed like a friendly man. I knew they were all trying to help me. I asked the paramedic to come over close to me.

"Could you slow down?" I asked. "Please slow down. I don't want to get into another accident. Please slow down."

He gave me a funny look. I don't remember his response. He probably tried to comfort me, telling me it would be OK and that we were almost at the trauma center. Not soon enough for me.

The long ride was bumpy. My ribs were killing me every time I breathed. My left hand was bandaged up with a splint. I wasn't too worried about it, even though I could not move it then, but it hurt to move my neck. The pain ran down to my legs and feet. But at least I could still wiggle my feet.

"Hey, can you please slow down?" I asked once again.

The paramedic just stared at me.

"No, really, can you slow down? I don't want to get in another accident. The roads are icy, please!"

No one reacted. I rolled my body to the side, pushed my head toward the driver, and politely shouted.

"Hey, can you please slow down?"

I will never forget the look on the driver's face. "We have to get you to the trauma center," the driver shouted back respectfully.

"Oh, please, slow down. I'm scared," I exclaimed. "I would rather die here than in another car wreck, please!"

To my relief, the driver did reduce his speed. I was so grateful. The roads were bad, and I just wanted to be safe.

I could feel the ambulance slowing down, making sharp turns, then suddenly stopping. The back door of the ambulance opened, and the paramedics told me we had arrived.

Heading toward the Roadhouse, I turned around to look at the truck. I could see the headlights of the crumpled-up white Chevy truck pointing toward me in the distance. Then I realized I might be going the wrong way. If I walked in the opposite direction of the headlights, I would be going back toward the Roadhouse. *Yes, that is it! I have the answer.* I was driving toward St. Mary's, and logic dictated I had to backtrack and walk past the truck to get back to the Roadhouse.

I felt the back and top of my head; blood was everywhere. I pushed myself to walk back toward the Roadhouse. My feet really hurt. Son of a bitch, the little gravel rocks pinched the sole of my foot every time I took a step. This road was not exactly the best place for walking barefoot; regardless of whether I had shoes on or not, I was not in the best condition for walking anywhere.

One foot in front of the other. My arms and hands were dangling down. The night was getting colder. I felt like I was going to freeze, being half-naked since most of my clothes had been torn, exposing several parts of my body to the elements.

Maybe if I run, that will warm me up, and I might have a chance of surviving.

"OK, go for it," I heard myself saying. God only knows. I started to run, faster and faster. I ran for what seemed like several minutes, and it became harder to catch my breath. My legs began to feel weak, and my foot was stinging. My gut was burning; it felt like it was on fire. The pain was unbearable, but I pressed on. I didn't know what to do. I didn't know how far I had gone or how long I had to travel to get help at the Roadhouse. It seemed as though I had ways to go.

Do I keep running or slow down and walk? If I continue to run, what will that do to my internal organs? I asked myself. *Did I damage them in that wreck? Oh, God, the pain is intense.*

I suddenly slowed to a walk. Maybe I was just out of breath. I wanted to turn around to see the truck's headlights, make sure I was heading in the right direction, and see how far I had gone. I was breathing very heavily, and the vapor from my breath surrounded my head as though I were in a cloud.

"Oh, God, help me!" I cried out. "Please, dear God. Am I dead or alive? If I am alive, then please do not let me die here. Not out here in the bush, please, not here. Not in this place out here. Let me die in Anchorage." *I knew I had miles to go, but I was unsure how long it would take.*

Feeling fatigued, my head was starting to drop. Only minutes had passed since the truck had overturned, but to me, it seemed like hours.

I haven't seen anybody on the road. Is everybody asleep? It doesn't seem too late in the evening; maybe it's around nine o'clock.

My head continued to droop downward. Glancing upward, I noticed a light moving up and down in the distance. *It must be a car! It must be coming my way. Thank God I am walking the right way.* Keeping my eyes focused on the light made me more fatigued; it was so hard to keep my head up.

Minutes passed, and the car wasn't even close. Oh man, the car is going the wrong way to St. Mary's. Just great. I knew I was dead meat if I sat down. It was all I could do to keep walking, more like hobbling. I was unable to look up, even when I heard an engine getting louder. Dust flew from behind a vehicle that screeched to a stop near me. The man driving the car jumped out, yelling, "Are you OK?"

I do not remember answering him. I was exhausted and having a hard time concentrating. He rushed over to me, grabbed around my waist and shoulders, and helped me into the car's back seat. He slammed the door shut, ran around the car, jumped in, and drove toward the Roadhouse. The pain was agonizing, but it helped that the car's heater was slowly warming me up.

After what seemed like a long time, I recognized the lights on the right-hand side of the road. The good old Roadhouse came into sight. I had made it! At least I had made it to the Roadhouse. I slumped down on a chair in the hallway. The next thing I knew, my co-workers were staring at me. I must have been a sight. A state trooper behind me started asking me all kinds of questions.

"Were you drinking tonight?" the trooper asked.

"No, I just fell asleep," I said in a fragile voice.

I could hear the work crew whispering among themselves. What were they talking about? I could see the biker plumber with his funny-looking mustache and beard talking to Yukon. Behind me, two young ladies who had just entered the building were staring at me.

"Somebody is going to have to take him to Bethel. He needs one of us to take him to the hospital," one of the workers commented.

When I looked down the hallway, I could see and hear the workers discussing who should take me to the hospital in Bethel, which was located around 101 air miles southeast.

"Well, I'm not going to take him," one of the workers shouted.

I could not believe what I heard. It must have been my imagination. Yukon walked toward me, bent over, and whispered into my ear.

"David, it's not you. It's because we all got stuck in Bethel for several months and nobody wants to go back there," he explained.

I couldn't believe what I was hearing. Even though I may have been dying, nobody wanted to take me to the hospital in Bethel. *Is this possible?* Discussed, right then and there, I knew for sure I was alive, no doubt about it, but for how much longer? The madness that surrounded me was ringing in my head. Par for the course. Just great.

"I don't want to take him," another worker stated.

"Hey! I know," another co-worker said. "Let's toss a coin. The loser has to take David to Bethel."

Oh my God! Why not just take me outside and throw me in the dumpster? The realities of bush life were hard and cruel. Apparently, Yukon lost the coin toss. How unfortunate for him.

Time flew by, and the next thing I knew, I was sitting in the back of a Cessna 206. Someone had wrapped blankets all around me. Yukon sat in front of me and continued to watch me as two pilots were taxiing for take-off. The engine roared, and I could feel the airplane vibrate as we rolled down the runway. The next thing I knew, we were up in the air. Yukon smiled at me and assured me that everything would be all right. Some thirty to forty minutes later, I could finally see the lights from Bethel, which looked like a big city compared to St. Mary's. Bethel's population at that time was around 3,600. It had some paved roads, including a hospital. The city's white, red, and green lights became brighter inside the cockpit. What a sight! The plane began to bounce around due to the turbulence we were encountering. Up and down, side to side, we bounced, and it hurt. The closer we got to Bethel, the more intense my pain was getting. I was shaking all over, and my teeth were chattering as if I were freezing.

"Yukon, I think I am dying."

"No, David, you're not. We're almost there. Just a few more minutes, we'll be landing," Yukon said with a warm smile. He always seemed to smile, even when he was unhappy.

"No way, I am not going to make it. No way," I cried out.

We continued to bounce around. The pain was getting more and more intense, and the numbness was fading quickly. Finally, I heard the rubber of the wheels touch down on the paved runway at Bethel Airport.

The pilot taxied the airplane to a tie-down where a cab was waiting for us. I was placed in the back seat of the cab next to two drunk men while Yukon sat in front. The cab driver seemed a bit nervous, but we finally got underway and headed toward the Bethel hospital. *Holy shit, what's with this road?* The frost heaves in Bethel were appalling. Up and down, we bounced while following the contours of the road. What a ride it was. The road was enough to shake a healthy person apart, let alone an injured one such as me.

"Ouch," I cried. "Slow down!"

"Oh boy, yes. I hope he lives," the taxi driver muttered anxiously. "Yes, let's drive slower."

The seat seemed to be as hard as a rock. Yukon looked back at me from time to time, checking to see if everything was OK as the two drunks became increasingly restless, talking loudly, even, shouting at times. They were slurring their words, so I couldn't understand what they were saying, but what did I care what they were saying? I was trying to survive. I wish they both would shut up.

I need this like I need a hole in the head, I thought. *This can't be real.*

Both men were swaying back and forth, and one of them kept banging into me. *What the heck? First, the bumpy road, and now this bullshit.* Getting knocked around by a couple of drunken strangers. Just more typical crap to deal with in the bush.

"Jesus Christ! Knock it off! Stop bumping into me, you bastards. What is wrong with you two?" I was pissed off, but with little or no energy to defend myself, I had no choice but to put up with it.

They continued to sway back and forth, babbling. They seemed pretty content with their behavior. "A land without mercy." I guess that would include people, too. *Shut up, Grandpa.*

The long trip on the frost-heaved road finally ended when we arrived at the Bethel hospital. Of course, the two drunk men were still talking very loudly, laughing, and bumping into my injured body, but at least the vehicle had come to a complete stop.

Thank God. Maybe I can get some relief. I hope the hospital has morphine. I did not care what kind of drugs I took. Now I wanted a lot of it. Hell, I would have taken a handful of anything just to escape these drunk bastards.

A wheelchair arrived at the rear of the taxicab. The taxi driver still seemed to be quite nervous, scolding the two drunken men as I remained wedged in the car. *Oh, God, let me out of here.* The door opened, and I could feel the freezing air of Bethel hit my skin. I began shaking even more; the pain was getting harder to deal with. Looking back on it now, I realize I must have been slowly coming out of shock. Every part of my body was in agonizing pain, and I was covered in new and old dried blood. When I was finally placed in the wheelchair and wheeled through the hospital doors, I felt a sense of relief. Thank God, I finally made it.

The Bethel hospital appeared to be a decent-sized care unit. They were probably equipped to handle most situations. Besides, Bethel Airport was equipped for jet services. Now, at least, I could get on a plane and get home rather quickly. *Soon!* Or so I thought. I passed through the hospital doors and heard them close behind me. I was wheeled to the front desk, where a nurse in a white uniform greeted me.

All right, I thought, *at least she is cute.*

To cope, I developed a strange sense of humor, even in the most brutal and bleak situations. It was that or cry. The nurse walked around the desk and took my pulse and blood pressure. She looked at me while continuing taking my vital signs.

"Do you feel like you're going to die?" she asked.

"I don't know, but I think so."

A moment passed and she gave me a strange look. *Why the hell is she looking at me like that? What's going on? Am I that bad?*

She looked at me again and said, "David, I have bad news for you." *Holy shit!* I thought. *I'm going to die out here in Bethel.*

"David," the nurse said, "we cannot admit you to this hospital." "What? I have insurance," I said in a loud voice.

"I cannot admit you because I don't believe you are going to die," she responded.

"What are you talking about? Look at me. I'm a mess."

"Yes, I know, but your blood pressure and pulse seem stable right now. You'll have to sit over there and wait for the doctor from the clinic to help you."

"What? What's going on? A doctor from the clinic? What the hell is this?" I shouted back at her.

"Hey, listen. Don't yell at me. This is a Native hospital, and unless we are sure you are about to die, we cannot admit you," she explained.

"What the hell are you talking about? Every minute, I get closer to death. You mean to tell me you won't help me?"

"Hey, don't complain to me. Write to your congressman," she said calmly. "Now, let's sit you over there to wait for the clinic's doctor." Man, she turned ugly fast.

First, the coin flip. Now this? I cannot get help. What happened to basic human rights? Even in my condition, I can't get help at this hospital. I guess I don't have enough blood on me.

I sat in that uncomfortable plastic seat for a long time, waiting for the doctor. I mean, it must have been at least two hours. Believe me, my mind was not playing tricks; there was a clock prominently displayed in front of me. For Christ's sake, no one cleaned me up. I was still bleeding, and blood was soaking through my head and shoulder bandages. As the blood dried, some of it flaked down onto the carpet.

Finally, I saw a man with a kind face walking toward me. It was the doctor from the clinic. They wheeled me to another area in the same hospital, where the doctor tried to fix me up as best he could with the limited tools he had. He put a few stitches throughout my head and wrapped my head up like a mummy. I cannot remember what else he did for me. I'm sure he cleaned me up somewhat, removing the dried blood as best he could from my face, hands, and legs. He gave me some pain pills and then sent me on my way to a hotel room, where I had to wait for the earliest flight out of Bethel. The medication did not come close to controlling the pain. The message from the crew was loud and clear: It was me who lost the coin flip.

CHAPTER 12
Cold Sweat

Move this way," the X-ray tech said.

I was dressed in a hospital unisex gown with no shoes or socks. The floor was cold. I had to stand while they took photos of my chest.

While standing, I used my right hand to keep my head up. I told the staff about it. They said not to worry and that they were going to take X-rays of my neck right after they were done taking pictures of my chest.

"Where am I?" I asked the person who was helping me. "Am I in the hospital?"

"No, that's in Kamloops," he said. "We're going to take you there as soon as we're done."

I told him I was cold. He brought me another blanket and I fell asleep. When I awoke, they had me lying in bed with my left arm and hand in a cast elevated above my stomach. As I shifted my eyes around, I could see other people lying in what appeared to be hospital beds in front of me. Though I *was hooked up to an IV, I was still struggling to breathe, remained in a lot of pain, and felt extremely tired. When I rolled my eyes to the right, I saw a nurse standing beside me. She looked at me and told me that I would be all right.*

"What happened to my hand?" I asked.

"They had to do reconstructive surgery," she said.

After establishing that I was in Kamloops, Canada, at the Royal Inland Hospital, I told the nurse I couldn't move my head. "I just can't do it," I said.

She advised me that the doctor would be in to discuss my injuries with me fairly soon.

MORNING FINALLY ARRIVED. Yukon helped me out of the chair. Then we waited in the lobby for a taxicab to pick us up and drive us to the Bethel Airport. My pain from the night before remained intense, and the blood and the soaked bandages made me even more uncomfortable. Tired and in pain, my thoughts were all over the map.

The cold air hit me like a ton of bricks as we walked out of the hotel toward the cab. *Oh, man, it's freezing. It is just too cold for me.* I walked toward the cab and all I could see was snow and ice.

"Everything will be all right," Yukon said with his usual smile.

I don't think it'll be all right, I thought, *especially if I have to get into that cab and take a long and miserable drive back to the airport.*

The road was rough enough to kill a healthy person. Yukon opened the back door, and to my relief, I had the whole back seat to myself. The driver was not in a rush, so the ride was not too bad, and there were no drunks to thrash me. Yukon was kind enough to stick around and see me board the aircraft for my flight home. I have always had great respect for Yukon, and I will always be grateful for what he did for me.

Finally, I boarded the aircraft. I had difficulty getting settled into my seat and putting on the seatbelt. I was thankful that I had pain pills, though I wished it was morphine or some other hardcore drug. By then, I would have loved to be knocked out; that would have been great.

The turbine engines spooled up to speed and were ready for takeoff. I could feel the vibration of the airplane as it lifted off the runway. I was on my way home.

The pain was unbelievable, but maybe now I have a chance to get some morphine anything for the pain. Exhausted from the whole ordeal, I couldn't sleep on the plane for some reason.

I kept asking myself, *Why was my life so upside down?* I examined my life, both the accomplishments and failures. At this point, I was only eighteen years old and already felt old and worn out.

I know the bush is beautiful and a way of life for many, but it's a hard one. And I didn't think I was tough enough to take any more. I have tremendous respect for anyone who lives in those conditions. But given the choice, I'll take the little things, emergency medical care and basic comfort over living off the grid any day. Maybe it's just me, but I think anybody would be pissed off if they were denied medical treatment, no matter the reason.

Will I always struggle in a place I do not want to be and never intend to live? Is this the way it's always going to be? If I am lucky enough to have children, will I miss most of their lives just for work? Will they be exposed to this kind of life? I knew I had to make a change, but I did not know how at the time. Not to mention, I was injured, which slowed me down.

It was hard for me to think.

I was so exhausted. I've got to try to sleep. Drugs, I need more drugs.

The aircraft's wheels squealed as they touched the asphalt at Anchorage International Airport. While departing the plane, I started to lose my faith in humanity. It was incomprehensible to endure such humiliation and disgraceful behavior. Even though I knew that most people were good, witnessing the rawness of what human beings were capable of doing is hard enough, let alone while you're injured. I was furious about the whole event. I said nothing to my stepfather until we got into his car.

"You could have gotten killed," my stepfather said when he saw me.

Exhausted, I answered, "Who cares? What difference would that make?"

I never told him what had happened to me because I knew he didn't want to hear it. He was dealing with his problems and now my injuries had added another burden to deal with.

It wasn't until later that I found out from the taxi driver who picked me up that I'd been walking in the wrong direction, away from the Road-house. Great, I thought. How the hell did I survive that? Someone upstairs must've been playing a sick joke on me.

I finally got to the doctor. The X-rays of my lower back showed a slight fracture. Like a football player's injury, he said, it was just a little hairline crack somewhere in the lower back. "You're going to heal up and recover from that injury."

My right shoulder was embedded with loads of gravel from sliding down the unpaved road. The flesh was ground down almost to the bone, leaving a five-inch circular gash. There wasn't anything the doctor could do for me unless I was interested in doing a skin graft, that is, where they take the skin off your behind and graft it onto your open wound area, which he warned would be much more painful than it is now.

"No way," I said.

The only thing they could do was bandage me up. Twice a day, I had to peel the blood-soaked gauze off, clean it up, and then put new gauze on it.

In addition, I had severely sprained my right ankle. "It would have been better if you had broken it. It's much easier for that to heal," the doctor said. "We'll wrap that up in a splint and you'll have some crutches for a while."

Healing up was excruciating because every time they peeled the gauze off of me and sprayed it with hydrogen peroxide, I would hop around the house a couple of times in pain. Not a fun time at all.

During this time, my stepfather was working on several HUD units in the Iliamna area. I did not put two and two together when he talked about the villages in Iliamna. That was the area we flew to for private and trophy fishing and hunting when we first moved to Alaska. At that time, I had no clue that Native villages existed in that area.

My stepdad was having a difficult time and decided to build at the start of winter. Building in the winter is extremely risky, especially in remote villages.

At that time, I kept hearing various stories about the bad weather and low morale. He needed help, so a little over a week after my accident, I started working at the Anchorage International Airport. Hobbling around with a sprained ankle and a big hole in my shoulder, I staged materials for the jobs, counting lumber and other housing materials needed for those projects.

Oh great, I kept thinking. *What the hell? I haven't even begun the recovery yet, and I have to work, but I loved that man; I desperately wanted to help.*

One evening, while lying in bed, I overheard my stepfather saying that somebody had passed away and he had to fly the body from Anchorage to Kotzebue. One of the pilots told him that when you fly a body in an airplane at high altitude, you can hear the body moan and groan because the lungs expand and contract as the plane changes altitude.

One day, at work, my uncle approached me and said we needed to do something. He did not tell me what it was. As we left the hangar, I saw my stepfather's 402 twin aircraft sitting on the tarmac. We headed toward the plane.

"What's going on?" I asked.

He told me we had to load an airplane. There were no boxes around the aircraft, and nothing was in sight, so I asked him again. What are we loading? He looked at me and then informed me that we had to wait here for a hearse because we were going to help load a casket onto the plane.

"What the hell!" I exclaimed. "I don't want anything to do with this."

The next thing I knew, a hearse pulled up and backed into position near the aircraft door. Two gentlemen wearing suits got out of the hearse, opened the back door, and started to slide a casket out. My uncle and I were freaked out. We stood on one side of the casket, the other two men stood on the other side, and we carried the casket to the airplane.

My uncle looked at me with a straight face to calm my nerves. "Relax, it's the cleanest thing you've touched all day," he said.

I am fairly sure he was as nervous as I was and was trying to make light of a stressful situation. As we lifted the casket to slide it between the double doors, the task became more stressful when it would not fit inside. We struggled several times, but it would not fit. There was only one way it would fit. The undertaker nervously instructed us to tilt the casket on its side.

As we rotated the casket on its side, we could feel and hear the body bouncing around inside the box while we were pushing and pulling to get it on the plane. It took some time to shift the casket in between the doors and onto the plane. Once we finally got the casket inside the airplane and into position, we had to rotate it so that it was right-side up. Oh God, I felt so, bad as the body slammed back over. The whole thing was traumatic for everyone, including both undertakers. I could see the head undertaker breaking into a cold sweat. The head guy took out his white handkerchief to wipe his forehead before reopening the casket to straighten out the body and retouch the makeup. The whole thing shook me up. It gave new meaning to "flying coffin."

Given what I'd been through, I thought that it could have been me lying in that box getting banged around. Holy cow, this is madness. I felt like I was losing my mind. Then I thought, once they land, they're going to have to remove the casket the same way we put it in. Jesus Christ, they're going to have to straighten up the body and fix the makeup again. As far as I know, the body made it to its destination, but I needed to move on from this and the rest of the stuff I had been through. I went right back to work, trying to keep it deep inside and not let it destroy my life.

Time moved very slowly, but it couldn't have been more than a couple of weeks before my stepfather came to me.

"I found Dirty Harry," he said. "I need you to go with me to hunt it."

Dirty Harry was the nickname for a big brown bear he had wanted to hunt for years. This was the granddaddy of bears for him, and he wanted it.

"What are you talking about?" I asked. "Even though I'm working, I can barely function."

"We need to get it," he insisted before leaving my room.

What the hell am I going to do? Is this a joke? I'm expected to go on a hunt right now? This is crazy.

I went into shock and got very depressed. *What kind of life do I have?* I kept asking myself. I felt as if the entire universe hated my existence.

CHAPTER 13

Lake Clark Pass

As I slowly opened my eyes, I saw a person in a white jacket standing on my left side.

"Hello, I am your doctor," he said.

Still unable to turn my head, I had to rotate my eyes out and down and to my left hand.

"What happened to my hand?"

"You shattered it, and I had to glue the bones back together and stick some pins in it," he replied.

I told him I was struggling to breathe.

"Yes, and it will be that way for quite a while because you broke your ribs."

"How many ribs did I break?"

He said that because there were so many broken ribs, they didn't count them. Oh my God. That's not good!

He also told me that I had crushed both of my calves and lacerated my liver. I mentioned that I couldn't move my head very well.

"It takes two hands to move my head back and forth," I explained.

"Well, that's because you had a very high-impact auto accident," he said, seemingly unconcerned.

I reminded him that I had been at the other hospital, and he said, "Yeah, that was the trauma center you were first sent to, and they did X-rays on your neck, and everything checked out OK."

What the hell? I asked myself after the doctor left.

I kept wondering if I would ever fully recover from this, and if so, what I would do for a living. Under a lot of stress and still in pain as well, I finally asked for more morphine. As I closed my eyes, I could see a glimpse of a dark road ahead and a giant trailer sliding sideways toward me.

MY STEPFATHER PLANNED to fly us to the hunting lodge near Lake Iliamna in the same white and green 185 floatplane he used north of the Arctic Circle. The next thing I knew, within a day or so of him telling me we were going on the hunt, he had already loaded the plane and was waiting for the weather to break. He had removed the floats and converted the aircraft to a taildragger, allowing it to take off and land on rugged terrain.

I remember my stepfather talking to me about how he had installed larger tires on the 185 so that he could land in sand and on various other surfaces, and had raised the propeller higher off the ground. Due to the rugged terrain, it is crucial to have the propeller higher off the ground, as it can occasionally come into contact with the ground during takeoff or landing, potentially damaging the blades. Getting rescued in the wilderness could take a long time, if at all, due to mechanical problems or some other mishap, which could be the difference between life and death. Search and rescue would have to fly through the same passes and weather that you just did, and they might have to delay searches by hours or days until the weather cleared up.

Our flight destination would be lengthy and risky this time of the year due to the unpredictable weather conditions. We were to fly through the rugged, mountainous Lake Clark Pass, one of the most hazardous passes at that time of year. It is located 284 miles southwest of Anchorage on the Alaska Peninsula and is the gateway to Katmai National Park and Preserve. This area is one of the best places in Alaska to observe grizzly bears in their natural habitat. And that's where Dirty Harry's home was.

The day we were to fly to our destination was cold, cloudy, and rainy with high, gusty winds, which made me very nervous.

Oh great, here I am, trying to recover from my accident with an open wound, and we are flying at the start of winter through a dangerous mountain pass that is probably going to have moderate to severe turbulence. Now I'm going to get bounced around in an airplane.

On top of that, we were still determining whether the pass would be open by the time we arrived at its entrance because the weather could turn from bad to worse and shut it down. Passes can be tricky to fly through because they can close up rapidly during your flight. Clouds can suddenly block your view of the mountains and the entire valley, disorienting pilots and occasionally making them fly into the mountains. Not only do you have to worry about clouds, but whiteouts can occur, which means the snow is so dense that you cannot see what's in front of you, causing the same effects as the cloud cover. Snow or sleet can easily attach to the top of the wings, propellers, and other surfaces, building up ice that reduces lift and stalls the airplane. In other words, the plane falls out of the sky. Ice buildup on rotating propellers can cause engine vibration and reduce power. Luckily for us, my stepfather's airplane had de-icing equipment on the front leading edge of the wings and propeller, but that was no guarantee of survivability.

Another dangerous element is high winds, especially updrafts and downdrafts shearing off from the mountains. While approaching the airport to land, pilots have slammed onto runways due to extreme downdrafts from the surrounding mountains.

Yeah, so there were many reasons to be nervous about this flight.

In Alaska, fatal plane crashes exceed the national average. Pilots must constantly assess the weather and terrain, look out for other aircraft in the area, and monitor their flight, fuel, engine temperature, oil pressure, RPM, and emergency landing areas. They also have to consider the safety of the people on board and have an exit plan in case the weather turns bad.

Pilots should drop their egos before boarding an airplane. As my flight instructor often told me, "If in doubt, don't." He had that note taped on all of his aircraft consoles.

While on that flight, I tried to take my mind off my worries by remembering how we would fly through Lake Clark Pass when I was younger to go fishing and hunting in the Iliamna area. I thought about our good times catching salmon, trout, dolly varden, and grayling.

Before going fishing or hunting, we usually prepare the plane the night before by loading up the gear and checking the engine. I got the privilege of fueling up the plane using the manual pump. The 185 held approximately eighty gallons, or 480 pounds, of fuel. I would have to push the lever up and down twenty-five cycles per five gallons. One cycle is pulling the handle down and pushing it back up. It takes about 425 cycles to fuel the plane. Gym? What gym? I had my own private outdoor fitness center. Sometimes, I would wash and wax the plane, including the underbelly; I would lie on my back and clean off the dark, gritty, exhaust soot from the engine. This would take some time and lots of elbow grease to clean off the grime. I used a special chemical that could cut through the grimy soot. I don't remember the cleaner's name, but I enjoyed using it because it smelled like bubblegum. Then, I would wax the entire bottom of the plane. Along with cleaning the plane, I assisted with various maintenance and preflight tasks, including checking the fuel for water, inspecting the oil, and draining water from the floats. The floats were in excellent condition, so there was minimal water to deal with. It was a great plane.

The next morning, we would get up at 3:00 a.m. and take off by 5:00 while watching the sun rise above the Chugach mountains, which was pretty amazing. We lived at the base of those mountains in Anchorage. On a clear day, we had a 360-degree view of the surrounding mountain ranges. From the southwest, we could see the start of the pass we were to fly through. We could even look north and see the mountain ranges leading up to Mount McKinley, which has been renamed Mount Denali, and is now back to Mount McKinley.

Located approximately 240 miles north of Anchorage, is the highest peak in North America, with an elevation of 20,310 feet above sea level. We lived on a hill about 700 feet above the city, which was nice because it allowed us to see the weather patterns from an elevated vantage point.

In my opinion, Lake Clark Pass is one of the most beautiful areas in Alaska and may be the most productive fishing and hunting area in the state. The entrance of the pass is about 120 air miles southwest of Anchorage, and the pass itself is around seventy miles.

The rugged terrain includes mountains such as Mount Redoubt, Mount Iliamna, and Mount Spurr, each towering over 10,000 feet. Many mountains have snowpack all summer, including many glaciers. Some glaciers have a deep blue tint, while others have a dirty, grimy color caused by rock debris that travels down the glacier in streaks.

When the sun is out and there is not a cloud in the sky, Alaska is one of the most incredible places on earth you've ever seen. You can't believe it when you fly through and see the peaks and valleys, how the sun lights up everything, and the brilliant colors show through. It is heavenly and makes you feel so good to be alive and excited by what the day offers.

My stepdad liked to fly high in Lake Clark Pass. The splendor of nature and all its beauty, jagged mountains with snowpack, valleys, waterfalls, and rivers, takes one's breath away. You see creation and nature at its very best.

Toward the end of the pass, the first of the larger lakes we fly over is the forty-mile-long Lake Clark, wedged in the valley between the mountains. It is about thirty miles north of Lake Iliamna and about 100 miles southwest of Anchorage.

Once we pass Lake Clark and go through the pass, the next lake to fly over is Lake Iliamna, the largest lake in Alaska and the seventh largest in the United States. It's around 1,000 square miles, 77 miles long, 22 miles wide, and has a depth of 988 feet. I saw it as a mile marker, for I knew we would be fishing in the rivers fairly soon. Lake Iliamna produces the most significant returns of sockeye salmon, more than any lake in the world.

Once we reached one of the large rivers, we witnessed a more impressive display of God's creation. As the bright sun burned through the airplane windows, flying around 300 to 500 feet above the river, we could see rows and rows and rows of large salmon lying on both sides of the river. Seeing millions of salmon traveling up the rivers to spawn is a hell of a sight.

We circled, looking for a landing spot on the river. While landing on rivers, pilots need to be on high alert for logs, as hitting one could turn a great day into a very bad one. We flew around a couple of times to look for the big game and check whether there were bears in the area. At that time, we did spot a bear downriver from us, so the trick was to fly a little further away from the bear. Even if you fly farther away from the sighted bears, they can still walk up to forty miles daily, so you must always be on your guard. That's why it's mandatory in Alaska to have a gun for your safety. We usually carried a .300 Magnum or a .458 rifle. We always wanted something big and powerful for safety, even though we were only going fishing, not hunting. Believe me, this is not for sport, it's for defense only.

I had always hoped animals wouldn't come to our location and try to snag our fish or attack us. We had to be careful about the wildlife because we caught fish in their territory. Besides looking out for bears, we also had to be on the lookout for a large moose or caribou herd entering our area. They could have calves with them, making them more dangerous. Heck, you might even come across a wolverine. Those things are vicious and could rip you apart. But even with those potential dangers, it was a lot of fun, especially knowing you would catch lots of salmon.

You must have the right equipment to catch salmon. Salmon are big and can weigh up to fifty pounds, depending on the type. Sockeye or pink salmon weigh anywhere from four to eighteen pounds. And it's much more challenging to catch fish in big flowing rivers. You have to consider the added current that the salmon use to get away from you. That is one of the many reasons to use high-quality, heavy-duty fishing poles and reels. Cheap ones tend to break, and you don't want that to happen while you're out in the middle of nowhere.

Usually, I would use an eighteen-pound monofilament line for salmon. That was the right pound line for me. If I used a lighter line, I often lost many lures by snapping the line on logs or rocks. On the other hand, if I used a heavier line such as twenty or higher, I wouldn't be able to cast as far as I liked, which would frustrate me.

It bothered me to see people use heavier fishing lines and bigger lures. I believed that was unfair to the fish. What was the point? We call those types of fishermen "meat fishers." They are only after the meat, not caring for the fish and the damage they can do if they snag it. Unfortunately, I have seen this many times.

The go-to lures I liked to use for fishing, including grayling, were flashy red and white daredevils on one side. The other lure I wanted to use was a flashy chrome pixie, with a red, pink, or green middle that looks like trout eggs. Depending on where we fished or what we were fishing for, we were not allowed to use real salmon or trout eggs to catch some fish. It was against the law.

My stepfather always respected law enforcement when it came to fish and wildlife. We always followed the law and kept a current fishing license on our person in case Fish and Game asked to see it. He taught me that they're a fantastic bunch of people who go around the state to ensure that people do the right thing regarding wildlife. And they were everywhere. You're in the middle of nowhere, thinking there's nobody around for miles, think again, an officer can sneak up on you anywhere.

My stepfather was very conscientious about being a conservationist when it came to wildlife. He taught me the benefits of catch-and-release fishing. He'd always say that if you release the fish back, you might catch it again, or someone else can. If people continue to catch them without releasing them, there will be no fish left.

"Don't waste the meat, eat all of it, or donate it to food banks," he would say.

The salmon we were about to catch would be eaten, so it was OK for us to keep our limit this time.

Most people wore rubberized, watertight hip waders while fishing in the rivers and lakes. This allowed the fisherman to maneuver in the water and escape the trees and bushes surrounding many waterways. Hip waders are necessary to wear, especially in a floatplane, so you can get on or off the floats to the shoreline to avoid getting your feet wet. The beauty of these boots is that you can roll them down below your knees while on the plane or boat, and when needed, they can be rolled back up to your hips and snapped to your belt. I never got the insulated hip waders, but at times, I wished I had, due to the freezing cold water. When you're wading in water for hours, it can be difficult to stay warm.

Another hazard is that if you wade too deep into a river with fast currents, you can easily lose your footing and get swept downstream. If the boots fill with water, there is a greater chance of drowning, so you must be careful. When we first moved to Alaska, I learned about this danger firsthand on my first goose hunt near a small town called Yakutat, located approximately 370 miles southeast of Anchorage, at the start of the Panhandle. It's an area fraught with bears, quicksand, and glacial rivers.

My stepfather had shot a goose that dropped out of the air around fifty yards away. He had to leave me alone for a few minutes so he could get his goose and told me not to move. Meanwhile, geese landed on the swift-moving glacial river next to me. I took my shot and got a goose, but didn't kill it. The river pushed the goose to a small sandbar about fifteen yards before me, where it continued to flop around. I was so proud of my shot and didn't want the goose to flop back into the river since I'd lose it if that happened. I did not want to disappoint my stepfather, so I stupidly decided to make my way into the rushing river, which proved to be much deeper than I had assumed.

I suddenly slipped into the freezing river, and my boots immediately filled up. I struggled to hold my head above the water, but my head submerged several times. I used my brand new .410 shotgun to keep from drowning and to push myself up and roll myself out of the river after barely making it to the sandbar. I lost my shotgun and lay on my back, thanking God I'd survived. I had come as close as one could to drowning or dying of hypothermia. As an eleven-year-old, I had to reflect on my foolish and ignorant actions that had put me in jeopardy. Pride came to mind. It was pride that almost cost me my life.

When my stepdad returned with his goose, he could see me soaking wet and freezing, lying on the sandbar near the goose I had shot. Now we had to get back to the mainland. I walked behind him, holding on to his belt through the icy river. The river water rose just below the tops of his hip waders as we slipped around on the rock below. It was a dicey situation. He never raised his voice; I could tell he was upset, but he showed no emotion. Having learned the lesson of self-preservation early on, I learned to take precautions.

Catching those big salmon in the high-current river was thrilling. Everybody had fish on, and we were catching them like flies. We all limited out fairly quickly, so we kept catching and releasing them back into the river throughout the morning. It was cool because there were so many

salmon that when you reeled in the lure, you actually could feel it bumping on top of the fish.

Happily, I only snagged one or two salmon that day. I don't like snag-
ging salmon or any fish of that sort because if the lure digs into the side of
the fish, it can be hard to remove it without damaging the fish. I didn't like
hurting the fish, especially if we were going to return them to the water.

Once we all had our fill of fish, we'd take off and fly to another place
through another pass surrounded by large, jagged mountains. He would
land near the lake's inlet, notable for its icy blue sheen, which he knew was
full of dolly-varden and trout. I preferred to use an eight-pound line for
those smaller types of fish, but many times, I would use a six-pound line.
Challenging myself to land them without breaking the line was fun.

On one of our trips, we saw a porcupine near the mouth of the river.
I kept a watchful eye on that porcupine while fishing. It had a large body
and was shaped like a round, pointy ball. I know males can weigh up to
thirty pounds, and this one was heavier than that. I could see the large,
sharp quills on that animal, which surprised me because I thought their
quills were much smaller. It kept walking around in the grass and on the
shoreline fairly close to us. It didn't seem too worried about human beings
in its habitat. It was so cool to see one so close.

I walked by myself about twenty yards from the mouth of the river
and cast into the lake, and it didn't take long before we were all into the
fish. It seemed like everyone was catching Dolly Vardens. People were yelling with excitement, "Fish on!" Completely satisfied, I kept one of those
fish and released the rest back into the lake. And why not? Because my goal
was to catch a big grayling. That is what I wanted, and I knew we had one
more spot to fly to that was loaded with grayling and trout. I can't remember how long we stayed on that lake, but it seemed like only thirty minutes
had passed before we all jumped into the plane for our next destination.

As we took off, I couldn't help but think of how beautiful that area
was and how diverse the terrain was, with its mix of rivers, mountains,

trees, and plains. What an incredible time to be alive. We gained altitude and leveled out. Flying through that pass, we saw the mountains piercing above the aircraft's height. My best guess is we were no more than 1,000 feet above the ground. Once we got out of the pass, it wasn't long before we could see the river on which to land.

After gathering up our fishing equipment, we walked a little through the trees following a bend in the river to the left. I was ready to go and had the proper tackle and rod just set up for this type of fishing, and to my great excitement, grayling and trout were jumping all over the river. I caught some trout, but they weren't the big ones I was looking for. Large trout in Alaska can get up to twenty pounds, but unfortunately, these trout were around twelve to fifteen pounds. I decided not to keep any of them because I knew I would come back someday, so I put them back in the river. Other fisherpersons were catching larger trout than the ones I had caught, but I was not deterred because I was seeking a big grayling.

Grayling, which can get up to twenty-four inches in length and around five pounds, is probably one of my favorite fish besides trout, because they are jumpers with big, beautiful dorsal fins and are just a lot of fun to catch. And, of course, graylings are really good to eat.

I continued to cast where they were jumping. Finally, I was catching grayling. The first couple was considered small, but they were still much bigger than the ones I had previously caught around Anchorage and at the cabin lake. I kept putting them back in the river, hoping to get a bigger fish. Finally, a nice, big one hit my line. It was a jumper, flopping all over the place on top of the water, so it was tricky to keep the line tight. As I landed it, I could see it was the biggest grayling I had ever caught at that time, about three pounds, and around sixteen to eighteen inches long. It was not as large as I had seen my stepfather catch, but regardless of the size, I just loved catching that fish, so I kept it.

I enjoyed reminiscing about those exciting times fishing on the lakes, but now it was winter, and I was injured, and we were on our way to find

Dirty Harry. As we climbed into the airplane and started to fasten our seatbelts, my stepfather turned to me and told me that we needed to use shoulder harnesses. This shocked me. After all these years of flying with him, he'd never told me to put on a shoulder harness before. This would not be a fun flight, not in the slightest. He was an excellent bush pilot and knew what he was doing; I had complete faith in him. Nevertheless, I was a nervous wreck.

He started the engine and checked all the controls as we taxied out to the paved runway. I noticed that the airplane was much higher than before, because of the larger tundra tires he had installed on the plane. As we took off and looked down at the landing gear, I could see from the weight of those larger tires that the landing gear had dropped significantly downwards. Having never seen those tires before, I kept thinking, *'Wow, those are large, heavy tires.'* I was glad that he had gotten them for the type of bush flying he wanted to do.

As we gained altitude, things were fairly smooth. It wasn't that bumpy at all until we started getting close to the entrance of Lake Clark Pass. There were scattered snow showers on the aircraft's left side, but not too much directly in front of us. The tops of the mountain peaks were shrouded in cloud cover. We both continued to scan the area for other aircraft and saw nothing.

Once inside the pass, the turbulence started to hit. He kept flying at the standard cruise speed and a safe altitude. He taught me how to make turns in passes safely, especially in bad weather. He explained how to align the airplane, allowing you to peek around each corner and look for a wall of clouds you can't fly through. Regardless of whether the pass remains open or closes up, a pilot must have an escape route to make a 180-degree return trip safely. Twenty minutes into the pass, the winds were picking up, and the clouds were creeping down the mountaintops. We were unsure if we could make it through the pass.

My mind wandered, and I started remembering our past caribou trips. I enjoyed my time with him flying through the pass and around the massive Lake Iliamna, scouting for caribou while he flew 500 feet above the ground.

"This is a perfect elevation when looking for animals," he'd explained.

We spotted some bears and a large number of caribou. Once we found the caribou we were interested in, we needed to find a lake to land on and set up camp. As I've already mentioned, Alaska has more than three million lakes, so finding a lake was no problem.

After landing on the lake and securing the floatplane, we would then set up the tent and make a campfire. At that time, it was against the law to fly and shoot the same day, so we'd always spend the night and get up early the next morning for our hunts. His campfires were fun because he'd show me how to make a campfire using Blazo, which he always brought. He would usually cut an aluminum Pepsi can in half and fill it with Blazo until it was full. Then, he would stick the can underneath the wood starter sticks and light it. He would smile as we watched a large blaze of flames engulf the starter sticks. I remember we'd had fishing poles, but we didn't go fishing. He'd brought those along in case we ran out of food.

Early the next morning, there was not a cloud in the sky, and we could tell it would be a hot day. We ate a cold breakfast, cleaned the camp, rolled up the sleeping bags, and put them back into the tent. He taught me that the food provisions had to be stored far away from the tent because of bears. Then he explained that if you keep the food in a tent, bears and other animals could tear it up in search of food. Not only could they destroy the gear, but they might eat all the provisions, leaving you with no shelter or food. I wondered if that had ever happened to him or his friends.

After everything was secured, we started our hike, looking for caribou. We each carried almost empty backpacks containing some food, mostly granola bars and bottled water, along with our rifles and ammunition. Even though we had flown in on the floatplane, our footwear was hiking boots; however, we had waders on board the plane, just in case they were needed. We hiked for hours and canvassed the area for caribou.

There were many caribou as we hiked, but none were the right size, or if they were the right size, they were too far away for us to get. An average bull caribou can weigh anywhere from 350 to 400 pounds, but can get up to 700 pounds. These animals are agile and fast. They make us humans seem like slugs as we try to navigate the tundra.

Tundra typically grows in areas where there is a lack of trees. Scientists don't know why that is. The lack of trees exposed us just about everywhere we went. There were no hiding places unless we could lie down on a little knoll, and the caribou were below us. Many times, we'd have to lie on our bellies to try to hide from the caribou.

Finally, that afternoon, we spotted some male caribou, which were the size we were looking for. The sun burned down on us; there were no clouds in the sky, and the winds were calm. A small caribou herd stood on a little knoll near a small lake. Perfect! We approached them slowly, crouched low, stopping often when we thought they might see or smell us. Like most animals in Alaska, caribou are wary of predators and can hear, see, and smell animals approaching them, especially people.

We took our time and bagged two animals when we got close enough. Both were clean shots, and we didn't have to track them. My stepfather began cleaning them and removing the horns. To keep the meat clean and unspoiled, we had brought many heavy-duty garbage bags in our backpacks, so we put the meat in the bags and hiked it down to a nearby small lake.

"Is that lake too small for you to land in?" I asked.

"No, not a problem," he replied as I continued to pack, carrying the meat to the lake.

I don't know how long it took, but he had to walk back to camp, roll up the tent, and put all the equipment back into the airplane. He also had a couple of five-gallon cans of aviation fuel on board, so he emptied those into the fuel tanks.

As I walked to get the remaining caribou, I could hear the roar of his 185 taking off. Within a few minutes, I saw him fly overhead and land on the little lake while I was taking the last load of meat. Once he landed, we loaded the meat into the airplane. The law then was that we had to carry the meat out first, and then the horns were the last to be moved. That was a good law because if people took the horns out first, they might leave the meat, which would indicate that they were poaching the animals for trophies.

We loaded the horns in the plane and took off, flying back through Lake Clark Pass to Anchorage, our home. What a great couple of days - so much fun! This was one of many good times that I remembered, but this trip to find Dirty Harry would not fall into that category, starting with the flight itself.

As the winds continued to pick up, the clouds were now halfway down the mountaintops. Just before the next turn, without warning, he reduced the power and lowered the flaps. Once the plane slowed, he adjusted the power and kept his hand on the throttle. He quickly explained why he did that and was preparing a turnaround. The cloud ceiling was lower as we looked around the corner, but it was open just enough to fly under the clouds. While turning, he lowered the nose and flew us under the cloud ceiling. It was one hell of a bumpy ride.

Oh boy, I thought. *We are going to have to do a 180-degree turn.*

Fortunately, the clouds were still high enough above the ground for an adequate margin of safety. We flew using Visual Flight Rules (VFR) and could not fly into the clouds, unlike commercial flights that use Instrument Flight Rules (IFR). Even though he was a proficient IFR-rated pilot in this case, it was VFR to the end of our destination.

I could not indulge in pleasant thoughts to keep my mind off what was happening because I was concentrating on looking for obstructions and other aircraft. On top of that, the further into the pass we got, the more turbulence we had to endure. Finally, to my relief, we were out of the pass and headed toward Lake Iliamna, a milestone point of our trip, which meant we were more than halfway there.

As we passed on the left-hand side of the lake, I could see wave after wave of large white caps. It was blowing like crazy, and we were getting bounced around. The shoulder harness pinning my upper body kept rubbing my injured shoulder back and forth on the seat. I kept wondering how much blood was oozing out of my shoulder, keeping in mind that I still had a lot of gravel in that open wound. Once in a while, somebody would find a piece of gravel and dig it out, but for the most part, it was pretty grim. Someone's going to have to patch me up when we land. *God, I hope we land soon.*

Some time passed, and we flew over the barren tundra plains without a tree in sight. Looking at the small lakes, I could see water blowing out of them, spraying several feet out onto the tundra. I had never seen that before while in the air, and it freaked me out quite a bit. I don't know how hard the wind was blowing, but try to imagine water being sprayed out of a lake by the wind's power. It resembled the images seen on the news cast during a hurricane.

Christ, when are we going to land? I asked myself again.

Finally, we were in radio range of the lodge, and my stepfather announced we were coming in for a landing and needed help with the airplane once we landed. He reduced the power but did not lower the flaps during our downwind approach, meaning we were positioned on the left side, parallel to the runway, about a quarter mile out.

This was the fastest approach I've ever witnessed. We were moving across the ground at a rapid pace. Still, with no flaps, he turned left perpendicular to the runway for the base leg of the approach while fighting the high gusty winds and turbulence. He turned left again for a short final and then put the flaps down 20 degrees. I distinctly remember that as we turned to the final approach, it was like slamming into a wall. As I looked down, it seemed as if we were almost at a dead stop, hovering above the ground.

The runway, well, it's not a runway. It's just a sandy area away from the tundra, nothing more than a little sand patch to land on. As we drew closer and closer to the ground, I could see several people standing on the right and left sides of the plane while we were virtually hovering over the runway. As we descended to about five feet above the landing area, he reached over to the flap handle and pulled it back for full flaps.

Suddenly, the aircraft rose rapidly into the air. I don't know how many feet we gained in altitude, but it was pretty high. My stepfather calmly applied more power to the engine, and to control our descent, he throttled the engine's power to control our rate of descent while controlling the elevators. The nose of the aircraft was pitched high as we hovered over the landing strip. He continued to throttle the engine to a safe landing.

Once we touched the ground, we rolled no more than three feet. He pulled the power, and I saw two men on each side of the plane grabbing hold of the struts and the wingtip ropes. They were hanging on hard because the wind alone could lift the plane into the air like a kite. He chopped the power off right away, and everybody smiled and laughed while guiding the plane to the tie-downs.

CHAPTER 14
Bear No Hide

"Do you know when I'll be released?" I asked the nurse who had come in to check on me.

She stared at me before saying, "There's a problem with your insurance. You owe the hospital over $12,500 and the insurance is unwilling to pay. We won't be able to release you till that's paid in full."

"What are you talking about?" I exclaimed with the little energy I had left. "I have car insurance."

"You need to contact your insurance company before we can release you," she insisted.

I couldn't look at her anymore and I stared straight forward and started to cry. You have to be kidding. What kind of a life is this? I was so disgusted. How could someone say such a thing?

I looked down and saw the end of my feet inside the blankets. I couldn't turn my head in any direction unless I used my uninjured right hand.

When I moved my eyes to the left, I saw that my left hand had been band-aged and splinted. I couldn't move my fingers at all.

WHEN WE GOT OUT of the airplane on my stepdad's quest to find Dirty Harry, it was windy as hell. This was a desolate area where the wind could blow so hard that sand granules could blast the paint off equipment and airplanes. It was raining slightly, but the wind's velocity made it seem like it was raining more than it was. From the air, I hadn't seen any trees. Most of the area was covered in tundra, with patches of sand scattered through-out. It seemed swampy, but I wasn't sure. I couldn't wait to lie down in-side as we headed to the lodge. I was in so much pain, my shoulder was aching like crazy, and my lower back wasn't much better.

How much blood have I lost? I wondered. *We're a long way from civi-lization. If someone gets hurt out here, it will take a long time to get back to a town with medical facilities.*

When we arrived at the hunting lodge, I was surprised to see it was much bigger than I had imagined, considering the location and the chal-lenges of accessing the area. Despite its weathered appearance, the rustic building was in reasonably good condition, with only a few areas showing signs of dilapidation. I wondered how the owner had been able to build this place, given all the materials that must have been flown in by small aircraft like ours.

Once we were inside, I was happy to discover that the place was warm. Everyone was friendly and happy, sharing stories of their hunting trips. I was pleased for them. I knew one of the gentlemen from Mexico, and I was glad to see him, but the rest of them were all new to me. We were finally shown our room. I quickly found the bed and lay down on my stomach so as not to bleed all over the sheets. That was all I could do, as frustrating and embarrassing as it was.

Unfortunately, my stepfather had to clean my wound. I explained to him that he'd have to soak the dressing in hydrogen peroxide before removing it, as the gauze was saturated with blood and would tend to stick to the open wound. When he slowly peeled off the blood-soaked gauze, I could hear and feel it tearing off the open wound. The pain was horrific. I didn't want to embarrass myself in front of my stepfather, so I just clenched my teeth and took it. Plus, I was so damn tired that I couldn't even move anyway. Once he cleaned me up, I fell asleep.

As far as I can remember, my stepfather never slept in, so we were up early the next morning. Some people were getting ready to fly out for their hunts. They would then gather up their gear, and a pilot would fly them to where a bear had been spotted. They would then spend the night with their guides and start hunting the next day.

They were using Super Cubs. A small, two-seat plane, the Super Cub is considered one of Alaska's best bush planes due to its lightweight design, heavy-duty strength, short takeoff and landing capabilities, maneuverability, slow flight characteristics, and low fuel consumption. They can go just about anywhere in Alaska, winter or summer, because they can be converted to floats, wheels, and skis.

The Super Cubs were tied down near the airfield/sand field and equipped with large balloon tires that resembled large, bouncing balls. They looked larger compared to my stepfather's 185 tires, but Super Cubs are a much smaller airplane. Since the Super Cubs are two-seaters and carry smaller payloads, pilots often make multiple trips to transport the guides and equipment to their hunting location.

Before we had breakfast, my stepfather again had to clean up my open wound, using similar techniques with hydrogen peroxide, and then apply new gauze. After breakfast, we went outside. I noticed it was cloudy, but the wind had died down significantly, and it wasn't raining. I didn't know what was happening until I saw people at the shooting range near the runway. This is where people would practice shooting, make sure the rifles were properly firing, and sight in their scopes. I'm guessing the guides also observed their clients to see what kind of shots they were taking into bear country. I mean, they were going out to face a ferocious animal that is fully capable of killing a human being without breaking much of a sweat.

My stepfather had a powerful open-sight .458 rifle, which he used as a backup rifle, with 550-grain bullets to knock down bears at close range. He would mainly rely on his .300 Winchester Magnum scoped rifle, which is more of a sports-type rifle used for longer ranges that can knock down bears. Though I preferred the powerful .458 rifle for backup, I really liked the .300 Magnum. It is truly a beautiful rifle.

These are high-powered rifles, and you have to hold them tight to your shoulder when you fire. Sometimes, when I practiced with the .300, I'd end up with black-and-blue marks on my shoulder from the powerful recoil. As my stepfather set up to practice, I kept thinking, *Oh, great. This is a perfect opportunity for him to ensure the sights and scope are properly dialed in for both rifles.*

First, he fired the .458 at the targets. The sights were dialed in for that rifle as he hit his target. He took two or three shots and then felt confident with the rifle. That rifle is so loud and powerful that each shot would reverberate through your body. He seemed to be enjoying himself, and so was everyone. Once he had fired his rifle, he turned to me and handed me the .300 Winchester Magnum.

"I can't shoot in my condition," I told him. "I can't do this, there's no way."

"Yeah, you can. Just do it."

"What are you talking about? I can't do this because of my injury."

"You can," he kept saying.

At that point, I wasn't sure I was going on the hunt with him, so as not to embarrass him in front of his friends. I grabbed the rifle and pressed as tightly as I could onto my right shoulder. It just so happened that the open wound was on the back of my right shoulder. I was afraid I might break my shoulder after shooting this rifle. I was wearing an oversized brown Carhartt jacket, which was thick and padded, but I didn't think that padding would be enough to protect my shoulder.

I lined up the rifle with the target and shot. Boom! I missed the target. My shoulder was killing me.

"You missed the target," he said as I turned to him.

"I know. I can't do this."

"Yes, you can," he insisted again.

I lined everything up, holding it as tight as I could to my shoulder. I squeezed the trigger and hit the target. When I told him I was done, he grabbed the rifle, shot it a couple more times and made some adjustments to the scope. He seemed very pleased now that the scope had been adjusted. I don't remember saying anything. I just returned to the lodge to lie on the bed.

Later that afternoon, my stepfather came into the room and told me to get ready to go. They found Dirty Harry, so we had to go right then. Groggy, not really understanding what was going on, and still reeling from the pain after shooting the rifle, I slowly got up and got my gear together.

How am I going to do this? How am I going to go out there and sleep in a little tent and sleep on rugged terrain with my injuries?

I found myself growing increasingly worried about it, especially after I noticed it was raining. *Oh great, it's going to be soaking wet and cold.* I had been told to put on my waders, so I did, along with my rain pants and jacket. Once outside, I walked toward the 185.

"What are you doing?" my stepfather asked me.

"I'm here to help load up the plane."

"No, we're not taking that, we're going in the Super Cub," he said with a smile. "I'm going out first to start setting up the camp. The pilot will bring in supplies, and you will go on one of his trips."

Watching him put the gear in the Super Cub, I noticed the wind had picked up. It wasn't nearly as windy as yesterday, but it was still windy enough. He and the pilot climbed into the plane and took off. Super Cubs, with their high-lift wings, can carry just over 800 pounds, take off in approximately 400 feet, and land in under 300 feet, even operating within their gross weight limit of 1,500 pounds or more. This exceptional capability empowers skilled pilots to navigate shorter and rougher terrains more easily than most other aircraft.

Nobody had told me where they were going and how long it would take to get back, so I walked back to the lodge and sat in the waiting area. I waited quite a while before being told the pilot was coming in for landing. I put my rain gear, including hip waders, back on and went outside to wait. The sun was starting to go down, and with the cloud cover, it wouldn't take long before we were going to lose light. When the pilot landed, he shut off the engine and waved me over. He was in a rush to get going because night was closing in. We loaded the plane with the remaining necessary supplies and took off immediately.

I knew one thing: Our camp couldn't have been too far away from the lodge because the pilot could not fly at night. As we kept flying, the terrain looked familiar: relatively flat, desolate tundra with some small sand dunes. Still, I thought that something seemed a little different about the tundra. It looked like a swamp. A better way to put it is that it appeared to be flooded.

Still having no clue where our destination was and how long it would take, I distracted myself and kept looking for wildlife—caribou, moose, bears. To my surprise, I saw no signs of life. That was baffling to me. I would have thought by now I would have seen an animal of some sort, but there was nothing. Looking out the right side of the Super Cub's window, I could see a tent and my stepfather walking around the camp area just ahead of us. We flew over the camp and the pilot slowed the plane down, turned left, and circled back around. As the pilot was setting up for his final approach, I kept looking out and asking myself where the hell we were going to land. The water was flooded all around the area, except for a small patch where the camp was, which was on a tiny knoll, if you could even call it that. It was more like a little hump. It couldn't have been more than 300-400 feet long and maybe 30 feet wide.

We would be camping in the middle of a tundra swamp, and it was raining. The good thing was that the wind was blowing in our direction for landing. As we descended, I could see the swamp water quickly coming from the tundra. The big balloon wheels touched down about ten feet past the waterline and bounced around quite a bit until we stopped approximately thirty feet from the other edge of the waterline. The pilot turned the airplane around 180 degrees and taxied to the tent that was in the middle. This was the first time I had landed on what I guess you could call a tundra island.

Once we got out and unloaded the plane, the pilot was somewhat concerned because he had to come back and get us the following day if we bagged the bear. If it continued to rain, the camp might get flooded and he would have no place to land.

"Oh great, I thought. A possibly flooded tent for the night, a broken body, and now it's time to go hunt something with teeth. What could possibly go wrong?"

Why was I out there in my severely injured condition? I don't know what the heck I was trying to do, impress somebody or what? I mean, how did I get talked into this? Of course, I wanted to go after Dirty Harry. We had been talking about that bear for a long time, but not like this, not by any stretch of the imagination.

After we unloaded our gear, the pilot spoke with us for a few more minutes while I continued to look around. We were truly out in the middle of nowhere, not a tree in sight, surrounded by water and lumpy tundra. He was in a rush to go, so he started up the airplane and drove it to the very end of the so-called tundra island. His wheels touched the water as he did a 180-degree turn back toward us for takeoff. I could see he held his brakes firmly as he started to add power, because the plane was not moving and water was spraying up behind him. Once the engine reached full power, he released the brakes. About 150 feet before his plane reached the water on the other side, the nose popped up, and he was on his way back to the lodge.

It was starting to get dark rather quickly, and I was exhausted. My bandage needed to be changed. At least the tent was dry, and we slept on thin, half-inch camping mattresses. It's hard to explain what tundra feels like, but it's grassy, lumpy, and spongy. In short, it's very uncomfortable to sleep on because it's not flat, and you have to sleep with the shape of the tundra. It is like a bunch of tiny hills ranging from six to fourteen inches high. Walking in the tundra can be tricky and difficult. It is a challenge, to say the least.

That night, I was so tired that I quickly fell asleep on the lumpy contours. I woke up in the middle of the night a couple of times, and I kept hearing the rain. I wondered if we would get flooded out. Being too tired and in excessive pain, I didn't unzip the tent to take a look.

The next morning, we awoke to more rain. It was raining even harder than the day before, and the water had risen slightly more overnight. I was expecting a very wet and uncomfortable day.

Along with our hip waders and all of our rain gear, backpacks, and our two rifles, we headed out into the open tundra swamp. My stepfather led the way, and I walked right behind him. It was tough going right from the get-go, up and down, walking on top of the lumpy tundra while sloshing in the water. Many places we stepped were so deep that the water would almost reach the tops of the waders. That made me more uneasy.

We kept walking through the constant rain with nothing in sight. The rifle was getting heavy, and the backpack was causing me lots of problems with my shoulder and lower back. Finally, we saw something in the distance. It was hard to make out, but it appeared to be an animal running and jumping. Eventually, I realized it was a bear, and it looked like it was playing and having fun.

We had to get a closer look. We hunched over with all the gear and quietly and carefully walked in the swamp, making sure not to splash water. We finally got into a position where my stepfather could look through his binoculars. Suddenly, he smiled.

"That's Dirty Harry," he said.

My heart started to pound.

We kept crouching, walking quietly, and moving toward the bear. The bear was still running around, jumping, and splashing in the water. As we got closer, we stopped on top of a tiny tundra mound that wasn't any bigger than five or six feet wide and just above the waterline. This allowed us to crouch down on our knees and stare at the bear.

The constant drizzle made it hard to determine which way the wind was blowing. My stepfather reached into his pocket and pulled out a box of matches. He lit one of the matches, then blew it out and watched the smoke, indicating the direction of the wind, which was blowing toward us. That meant that we were downwind from the bear. I had never seen him do this before.

"Remember what I told you," he said in a low voice. "Bears can smell animals downwind from them. This will be difficult, so we need to walk more slowly and quietly."

Fully exposed, we hunched over toward the bear; we would take a few steps and then stand still. Take a few more steps and stop. This went on for approximately ten minutes. Finally, we were close enough to get a shot. We were about twenty yards from the bear as it was still running around, not paying attention to us. It really looked like he was playing. Even though the bear was massively large, hitting a moving target was a bit more challenging. Crouched over, I quietly had the target in sight.

Suddenly, the bear turned its entire body toward us and stood on its hind legs. He was massive every bit as huge as people said he was. Still, I wasn't panicked, probably in part because I was in too much pain to be worried about getting mauled by the bear and partly because I was with my stepfather, who knew what he was doing. He had the backup .458 rifle, which made me feel much better. Even though I was using the .300 Magnum, I still wanted that backup, just in case.

The bear crouched back down, started walking, stood up on his hind legs again, and stared at us. We stayed completely still. From my days in Kiana, I had been taught that bears cannot see very far and can't see in color, so I figured we looked like two blurry bushes. *So, the bear doesn't know what we are*, I thought. *Plus, we're downwind.*

The bear stared at us, then abruptly plopped its front legs down, splashing the water, and ran off. My stepfather started to shake his head.

"Damn. The bear smelled us," he repeated over and over as he kept shaking his head. "He smelled us downwind."

Later, I discovered that bears do see in color. They have excellent eyesight and can see quite well. If that is true, which I believe it is, then it is pretty impressive that we managed to get so close to the bear while being fully exposed.

Once the bear left our line of sight, we turned around and tromped back to the camp. The walk was long and arduous. I kept falling behind due to my pain and exhaustion. Concentrating on each step I took, I eventually looked up and saw that my stepfather had come to a dead stop. I thought he was waiting for me. I slowly walked up toward him, and he started to crouch down as I approached him. "Do you see it?" he asked.

"I do. It's a big caribou."

It was the largest caribou I'd ever seen. The horns were pretty good size, but the body was huge.

"Get ready," he said. "You're going to get it."

"OK, if you want me to try, I will."

I really didn't want to get the caribou at all. I was only going to do it because he had asked me to. However, that body was so impressively large that I intended to mount it. I got down on one knee and lined up the rifle with the caribou about twenty-five yards before us. I aimed and fired. The caribou went down immediately.

"Wow, I'll say this for you," my stepdad said. "You're a hell of a good shot."

My stepfather immediately went to the caribou and cleaned it as quickly as possible. It wasn't easy because the body was so large, and half of it was submerged in water. I helped him roll the animal over back and forth to remove all the meat. It was a tedious and time-consuming task, made even harder by the swamp. "I'm going back to the camp to call for the pilot to come pick us up," my stepdad said once he had gotten the meat squared away. He stared at me. "It's your caribou. You shot him; you pack the meat." Then, he put his pack on his back and started walking back to the camp.

What? I thought to myself. *What the hell? What is going on here? Did I do something to piss him off? What the hell is he talking about? I can barely walk, let alone carry my rifle.* Not knowing what to do, I just stared at him as he walked away.

I couldn't see the camp, so I didn't know where we were. I just knew that it was getting late and that it was pouring rain. Because we were in bear territory, I was afraid to stay there alone, so I immediately grabbed my backpack, placed it over my left shoulder, and tried to follow him before he got out of sight.

I don't remember how long it was till I got to the camp or how I carried out all that meat and horns. The little bits and pieces I remember are that I kept stepping into deep holes that almost filled up my hip waders with water, and I nearly fell several times.

As I was bringing in the last meat, I saw that the plane had already landed. My father told me he was returning to the lodge with some of the meat. Because it was getting dark, they rapidly loaded the plane and took off. During their takeoff, I noticed that the little so-called tundra island we stayed on was almost submerged by water.

Oh, s**t, I thought. *How am I going to get out of here? I mean, how's the pilot going to land? It's flooded, and there is not enough room to land. I'm by myself with no tent and with caribou meat. After a while, I finally heard the airplane coming back.*

The pilot reduced the power and started his final approach. I moved off to the center of the mound and stood in water just above the top of my foot. When he landed, the main wheels dragged through the water. The plane slowed down as the wheels hit the top of the dry area and rolled to a complete stop, submerging the balloon tires in two to three inches of water. He quickly turned around, gunned the plane toward me, and shut down the engine. Then we loaded up the plane with the few remaining pieces of meat, my rifle, and me.

"Are we going to be OK?" I asked.

He started up the plane and drove it out as far as he could into the water without hitting the propeller. Then he revved up the engine to full power, water spraying everywhere from the propeller. As we approached the top of the hump, we were still on the ground. Once we reached the water's edge on the other side of the mound, the nose suddenly lifted and we were flying.

Well, that was an adventure, I thought. *I can't wait to get back and lie down.*

We made it back to the lodge by about four o'clock. I was in pretty bad shape. My shoulder was in constant pain, and I needed assistance to change my bandage. Blood had soaked through the bandage and stained the inside and outside of my coat. I was so tired, worn out, and in pain, I just wanted to get to bed once I got cleaned up. I walked to the kitchen to get a sip of water. As I turned around, the Mexican gentleman behind me started to talk to me in broken English. He told me they appreciated what I did and that he wanted to thank me for giving him my caribou hide. I stood there and stared at him for a moment.

"Oh, you're welcome," I finally said.

Then he told me that he had shot a caribou a couple of days before and that the horns were very large, but the body was small. He had seen my caribou and liked it because the body size fit what he wanted, so he asked my stepfather if he could take the skin. He continued to explain that his horns and my caribou hide would be mounted and then displayed in his bar and restaurant in Mexico, a place I was familiar with because I had visited there a couple of times in the past.

What could I do? I had to say yes, obviously, but I wanted that caribou. I had to pack the damn thing while injured, and now someone else was taking it. I was not very happy. Exhausted, I just wanted to lie down.

The next morning, around ten o'clock, we loaded up the 185. I couldn't wait to leave. I wasn't hungry or anything; I was in so much pain, and I just wanted to get some medical attention when I got home. Once we took off and headed back, I kept thinking about carrying that damn caribou back to the camp with my wounded shoulder.

It was overcast, and the winds were considerably tamer than they had been over the past two days, so at least the flight was fine. After quite some time, we finally could see Lake Iliamna as we headed toward Lake Clark Pass. Looking down, I could see snow and ice everywhere. Iliamna Airport was right in front of us. My stepfather started to reduce the power and began to approach the paved runway. He didn't tell me what his plan was. The only thing I could think of was that he needed fuel to get through Lake Clark Pass.

Once we landed, we taxied toward one of the hangars on the right side. Then he turned the engine off.

"OK, let's go," he said.

As we exited the plane, I saw building materials spread all over the tarmac. The materials looked familiar; they were the items I had helped stage at the Anchorage airport. Looking up, I saw Brian. I hoped everything was going well for him. As I headed to the restroom, I could see they were talking. As much as I wanted to say hi to him, I didn't because I was hoping we would be taking off for home shortly. Sometimes these meetings could last hours. When I returned to the airplane, Brian called me over and started talking to me. Then, we all jumped into the truck and drove away from the airport. I kept wondering when we would leave. Little did I know that other plans were in store for me.

CHAPTER 15
Newhalen

A nurse walked in. "The insurance company's on the phone," she said.

"What insurance? What are you talking about?"

"They want to speak with you. I have to wheel you to the hallway."

You've got to be freaking kidding me, I thought.

I was twisted with pain, a burning catheter jammed inside me, and my bladder was screaming. Still, she hoisted me into a wheelchair and rolled me out.

When I got on the phone, I spoke with the insurance representative in the United States and asked him what was going on. They informed me that, due to Insurance Corporation of British Columbia (ICBC) policies, they weren't allowed to pay the bill because the accident occurred in the Canadian province of British Columbia (BC) and not in the United States. If this had taken place in the United States, about 158 miles from the border, it would be no problem. The insurance would kick in and everything would be taken care of.

"I don't understand what the hell's going on," I told him. "I have three insurances: my private insurance, that's you guys, my auto insurance, and my father's insurance on the truck."

"Yes, we understand all that," he said. "But the problem is, since it happened in BC, Canada, the ICBC government insurance company is supposed to pay for all the damages, no matter who is at fault. Once they pay, then our insurance company will reimburse them." "Yeah, but they're not going to release me from the hospital," I stated.

"I understand, sir. I'm so sorry, but there's nothing we can do."

"What am I going to do?" I asked.

"I don't know what you're going to do. You have to talk to the ICBC insurance adjuster in Canada."

In a weakened condition and completely distressed, I hung up the phone and returned to the room. I thought I had already gone through hell out there in the villages. Now I had another type of hell to deal with on top of all my physical damage and mental distress. I kept having those flashbacks of the dark road and the truck hitting me.

THE ROAD WE TRAVELED on was unpaved. As my stepdad and Brian continued to talk about business and how the jobs were going, I just kept staring out the window, wondering where we were headed. Brian made a right-hand turn onto a bumpy off-road trail. I don't even know if you could call it a trail, but we were driving on top of the tundra in ruts carved out by old tire tracks. The little truck kept sliding back and forth due to the ice and snow on the road. As I looked up ahead, I saw a long, dirty white canvas dome tent just before us, a Single-Truss Arch Storage about 30 x 65 x 15 feet. Once we got closer, I could see a whole bunch of things lying around the outside of it.

What's this? I wondered. *Perhaps he's using it for storage or something else.*

The truck came to a stop in front of the tent. As we exited, I noticed that people were going in and out of a plywood door on the front of the dome tent. Thanks to a self-closing spring, the door made a loud bang as it closed.

Although it was only September, it was cold, cold enough to keep the snow frozen but wet. In other words, it was pretty sloppy and icy. I turned to Brian.

"Where are we?" I asked.

"Welcome to Newhalen," he said.

A gentleman greeted me as I opened the door and walked into the tent. "Hello there, how are you? Would you like some cookies?" He showed me to the makeshift kitchen that ran along both sides of the door. They'd set up tables to store food, utensils, plates, and cookware. Looking around, I could see a stove in the middle of the tent with the flue rising up and out of the tent. Just in front of the stove, I saw tables and chairs that looked like the dining area for what I guessed was the crew.

I moved around and heard the clinking of my shoes on the wooden floor. This seemed odd to me. Then, I noticed empty cots along both sides of the tent running past the stove, almost to the start of the kitchen's stored supplies. Turning around, I saw Brian carrying items, including my small bag. Some of the crew entered the tent and sat down at the table. Brian was talking to them, and then he turned to me and announced, "Now you're the runner."

Runner? What is he talking about? I can't run; I can hardly get around. What's a runner?

He just stared at me and smiled.

"I don't understand," I said.

"You're the runner," he repeated before I could ask him again what a runner was. Then he and my stepfather jumped into the truck and left without saying anything to me.

Once again, I had no idea what was going on. I went over and started talking to the gentleman who had offered me some cookies. He told me that he was the camp cook and that he had some problems cooking because he wasn't getting the food he'd requested for the crew.

"What is this place?" I asked.

"It's the camp shack where we are staying."

"What?" I asked, "Staying in this tent?"

"Yes," he replied. "We are." Then he told me that the heating stove in the middle of the room wasn't working well. He mentioned that it might be out of oil, but he didn't know what was wrong with it.

"The boss needs to get that fixed immediately," I said.

"Yeah, it's freezing in here. It gets pretty cold at night," he told me.

As more people arrived and took their seats, he began to serve them food. I sat and ate what was on the plate, along with some of the cookies he had just made. Usually, the camp cooks made cookies for the crew to raise their morale by giving them a little taste of home. I longed for home and once again wondered what I had done wrong to deserve to be out here in my condition.

Did I piss off my stepfather and Brian? Are they mad at me because I got into an auto accident?

I was still trying to figure out the Dirty Harry fiasco. I kept wondering, *Why me? Why was I out there? Why did I have to go on that nightmare of a hunt and carry all that meat myself?*

I began praying to God, asking my real father to help me. *How do I get out of here? What do I do? Father, please, I'm injured. I need some help. Please help me.*

At that time, I carried only my jacket, rain gear, thin water boots, tennis shoes, some long-sleeved shirts, a thin pair of gloves, and a thin hat. I had no work clothes or proper winter gear for this place.

What the hell am I going to do? I kept wondering, *Jesus Christ, did I make the wrong decision and I die in that auto accident, now I'm in hell?*

I didn't tell the cook or anyone else about my condition; I just kept to myself. I went outside to use the bathroom facilities and found a small freezing outhouse for the crew. Then I realized there were no showers.

Where do we wash our hands and brush our teeth? I wondered. *Where are the restrooms? How do we maintain decent hygiene?* There was nothing in my line of sight, and there was nothing inside the tent. I stood outside the tent and surveyed the situation. We were almost in the middle of nowhere. Looking farther out, I could see a row of houses off in the distance.

That must be the village of Newhalen. So why are we sleeping in a tent? I thought. *This makes no sense. The town's right over there. Why aren't we staying in one of those homes?*

As I relieved myself outside, away from the camp tent, I could see more people going into it. When I made my way back and walked around the tent, I saw a fifty-five-gallon oil drum lying horizontally on a stand, with piping from the tank leading into the tent. It was common in Alaska to use oil tanks to fuel the heating systems.

Back inside, I sat at one of the tables and listened to people talk. What they had to say about the job wasn't too pleasant. I asked what villages they worked in. They told me they were building in four villages: Igiugig, Kokhanok, Newhalen, and Nondalton. The first three villages were located around Lake Iliamna. They were not happy and complained about the first three jobs in those villages.

Igiugig is about forty-four miles southwest of Newhalen on the other side of the lake. The small village has about sixty-five residents, comprising Yup'ik Eskimos, Aleuts, and Athabascan Indians. The town is well known for its rainbow trout that grow more than thirty inches. These were the big trout I'd been talking and dreaming about.

Kokhanok, nestled twenty miles south of Newhalen, hosts a diverse Native population, primarily Yup'ik Eskimo and Dena'ina. The average population is around 120 people.

Newhalen is about four miles south of the Iliamna airport. It is on the north shore of Lake Iliamna at the mouth of the Newhalen River. With a population of around 150, it has a mixture of Dena'ina, Yup'ik, and Sugpiaq cultures.

Nondalton has a population of around 123 people. It is situated on the west shore of Six Mile Lake, between Lake Clark and Lake Iliamna, about twenty-two miles north of Newhalen. Its Native culture is made up of Dena'ina Athabascan Indians.

Along with Lake Clark, these four villages and towns offer world-class fishing opportunities for salmon, trout, and grayling, as well as other rich wildlife experiences. But I wasn't here for fishing or the wildlife, that was for damn sure.

"What's happening? What's the problem?" I asked once I'd gotten the lay of the land.

They said they were having a difficult time obtaining the necessary materials to build. Some of the materials were placed far away from the job sites, so they had to drag them by hand to the sites. They also complained about the lodging conditions and the lack of shower and bathroom facilities.

"Hey, it is freezing in here," I said. "Did you run out of oil in the tank?" Someone told me the oil tank was full, but the regulator was broken. Suddenly, a couple of the crew members went over to the oil heating stove, banged on the regulator, examined it, and tried to figure out what was happening. Then, someone came up with the bright idea to remove the regulator and tie the piping directly to the stove, regulating the oil flow from the outside valve to control the flame. So, one person went outside and shut off the valve on the oil tank. Then, the small group around the oil stove removed the regulator and tied the piping directly into the furnace.

As I sat back and watched this unfold, people started suggesting it might not work, that it was a bad idea, and that the stove would catch on fire. Others were saying, "We'll just shut it off at the valve," "Don't worry about it," and "It's no problem at all." Once everything was connected, someone shouted to the person outside to slowly turn the valve on. Then another person went ahead and lit the stove. A big explosion of flames shot out of the stove and up the flue. They closed the door and everything seemed pretty good. So, they told the person outside to open the valve slightly more. As soon as they did that, a rumble began in the stove, growing louder and louder. The next thing we knew, the flue began to turn red, and the stove started jumping around the floor. "Shut it off!" some of the crew began to scream. "Shut it off! Shut off the valve!"

The person on the outside shut off the valve, but the stove continued to bounce around the floor, and the flue glowed a deeper red. I could feel the intense heat emanating from it, even at a distance of around fifteen feet. *Oh man, we're going to lose the tent.* I thought it would catch on fire, along with everyone else. People kept shouting, "Turn it off, turn it off!" Time seemed to slow down, and quite a while passed before the oil cleared out of the line. It then took a while for the stove to cool down. Once we finally knew we were safe, everyone in the tent started laughing. OK, so this was my first day in this camp.

I went outside for some fresh air, and off in the distance, I could see lights bouncing up and down and right to left. Eventually, I figured out that it was the little truck heading toward the camp. As it got closer, I saw some items in the back, including a gray garbage can. Two people were in the truck. I was happy to see my boss and uncle. I went up and talked to him. Before long, Brian approached us and said, "You're the runner. *What the f*** is a runner?* I kept thinking. You guys put this garbage can and all the other stuff inside the tent." When I looked inside the truck bed, I spotted a familiar duffel bag. "Hey, is this my duffel bag?" I exclaimed.

I was told it had been sitting at the airport. Apparently, a relative back in Anchorage had packed my clothing, winter gear, and boots and shipped them out for me.

Oh great, I thought. *I guess I am staying here to work. Just great!*

We put the tailgate down and started to lift the garbage can, which was super heavy.

"Jesus, what's in here, Uncle?" I exclaimed.

"That's our water for the camp," he said.

We had to lug that into the tent; otherwise, it would freeze overnight and be useless the next morning. We set it where the cook told us to. Then we grabbed all the other items from the truck and put them in the camp.

Since my uncle had just arrived, I asked him where he would be sleeping. He picked out a cot, so I chose one that was next to him because I needed help cleaning my wound every night. My uncle was gracious enough to assist me in that effort. We discussed the other villages and their problems, and then our conversation turned to him.

"You're putting on the roofs?" I asked.

"Yeah," he replied dejectedly. He wanted to be an electrician, so his goal had been to work with the sparky on the jobs. He was pretty down about installing roofs, despite being in charge of all the roofs. He was a gifted person and mastered everything he did. He laid things out and proceeded methodically in any job he was tasked with doing. He was truly a talented man. I never did discuss the bear hunt with him or anyone in the family. I was just too distressed about the whole situation.

Before we went to bed, my poor uncle had volunteered to clean off my bloody gauze. He soaked it with hydrogen peroxide and then peeled it off while I moaned the whole time because some of it ripped and tore, and I could hear it coming off my back. In addition to blood and pus and everything else, I still had a lot of gravel stuck in that open wound, some of which was slowly working its way out. Sometimes I tried to pick it out with my fingers.

Since the oil stove was not working at all, we had to sleep in the freezing cold, and of course, it got colder and colder as the night went on, dropping to subzero temperatures inside the tent. The bed consisted of an uncomfortable cot and a sleeping bag. All night, I kept tossing, turning, and shaking because I couldn't get warm. I lay wide awake, hour after hour, until it was time to get up. Finally, I heard people getting up and coughing and hacking, and of course, I could hear the cook banging around preparing breakfast.

I didn't know what time it was. I opened my eyes and looked up at the white canopy which was covered in ice chips. My sleeping bag was also covered in ice chips. I could see breath coming out of my mouth. As I unzipped my sleeping bag and put my foot down, I noticed the wooden floor was soaking wet with ice patches.

Oh, just great, it's going to be one of those days, I thought.

I got cleaned up for the day as best I could. I didn't brush my teeth or wash my face because I didn't know where to go since nobody had told me. Luckily, my uncle was there, thank goodness, so he could clean my wound again in the morning and patch my back up. Thankfully, the duffel bag sent to me was full of warm-weather gear, so at least I had insulated underwear, winter socks, my beaver hat, and my bunny boots. The military developed bunny boots for extreme cold weather. They were white, big, clumpy, not too heavy, fairly comfortable, and could keep your feet dry and warm. I was grateful to have them.

After breakfast, I was still unsure what to do, so I went outside to get some fresh air. I could see the sun coming up. A tall man with a beard and mustache walked up to me with his cold-weather jumpsuit on and a flashlight on his head. He looked funny, but he seemed nice and asked me to go with him.

"What are we going to do?"

"We're going to start our foundations and you're going to help me."

"How will we do that if the ground is frozen?"

"I'll show you."

He was carrying a pickaxe hoe, and we started walking.

"Where's the job site?" I asked.

It was right in front of us. He told me he had started laying some footings the other day. We walked to the building site, which was visible from the crew camp tent, but far enough away that you wished you had a ride, especially in the cold. Walking to the site was a challenge because we were walking on the same tundra I'd experienced during the hunting trip. However, it was icy, making it slippery as well as uneven and clunky. With a weakened right ankle, that certainly didn't make me too freaking happy.

I was familiar with the type of foundation being used at this job site. I had installed it when I was younger while working north of the Arctic Circle in Kotzebue during the summer months.

Once we laid out the stakes and squared everything up, he showed me how to install pads in the wintertime. He started digging the tundra using the pickaxe hoe. To my surprise, there wasn't so much digging as we had to scrape down the tundra to get the required four-by-four-foot pads level and square them for the flooring crew.

"They're going to sink into the ground," I said.

He told me he understood, but my job was to place these pads where they needed to go. "I don't worry about it because they're adjustable foundations," he said. Then he went over to the pad and asked me to help him lift it into place.

"I can't do that," I said. "I don't have the strength."

"Just help me get it up on edge. Then I'll roll it over into place."

We did that together for all the pads, then pushed them back and forth with pry bars until they were lined up in a straight line to install the floor system properly. Cold and wet, we continued to work throughout the day until sunset.

I was exhausted, damn cold, and my gloves were soaking wet from the icy snow. We wrapped up and headed to the camp.

"Where do we take showers?" I asked my workmate on our way back.

"Oh, we have to go to the gym."

"What do you mean, the gym?"

"The high school gym is the only place they will let us shower."

"So why are we sleeping in this tent?"

He explained that the locals were trying to extort money from our boss and were demanding a substantial amount for housing. He had refused to pay their fee, so now we were stuck out here in the tent.

"Oh, great," I said.

I went to my cot and lay down on my stomach because the wound in my back was causing me a lot of pain. I took off my boots. My socks were soaked through, not because of the wet and icy tundra, but because bunny boots are sealed up so tight your feet can't breathe. So, your socks get soaked with sweat.

As I lay there, more crew members began to arrive and eat. I was so tired, I grabbed a little bite and a cookie. My jacket was full of blood on the inside, so I turned it inside out to dry it. My uncle finally came back and patched up my wound again. This time it was really sticky and bloody, and it took him a little while to get the gauze off, such a nasty job. My shoulder smelled bad, and I needed to take a shower, but I was too tired to do so.

CHAPTER 16

Tiptoe Around

T he next time I woke, I saw a lady standing beside me. I could tell it wasn't a nurse because the person was wearing what I would consider civilian clothes. When she greeted me, I rolled my eyes toward her and started blinking. She stated that she was with ICBC, and there were some forms I had to sign.

"I'm not going to sign anything right now," I said.

"We have to do that."

"No, I'm not going to do that," I repeated. "I'm in too much pain, I can't think or do anything right now."

"What's going to happen is that your insurance will not pay for the damages, but the hospital will release you. Then you'll have to settle up with them later on."

"I still don't understand what's happening," I said.

She didn't offer any further explanation. Instead, she said, "I'll take you to an office and you can sign documents there. Then we'll get you out of here *as soon as the hospital releases you. We will get you a flight back to where you're from, and we can discuss the rest later on."*

I am over 2,000 miles from Anchorage. *I could barely comprehend the arrangements she had outlined.*

"You were in a head-on collision with a dual-trailer semi-truck," she said, adding that my brother-in-law was flying in to help me out.

Oh my God, I need to pay for his flight, *I thought.*

I didn't want him to spend his own money. He was such a nice guy. And I certainly didn't want my parents to spend their money on me.

Sometime later, the hospital administrator came into my room to discuss how they were going to release me from the hospital and that I needed to stay there for a few more days. I kept telling her I couldn't move my head without using my hands, but she never responded to that. I told her my vision was blurry, and again, she didn't say anything, just that they were going to release me soon and that I'd have to pay back the money to the hospital.

When she left, I started to cry once again.

Why? Why is this happening to me?

The sadness hit hard as I thought of my real father. I hadn't spoken to him in years, though I'd pleaded with God for help. But all I ever got was silence. He was gone and I was still here.

How can that be? He's dead, and I'm alive.

EVEN THOUGH IT was pitch black outside in Newhalen, it was still fairly early. I guessed around eight o'clock. Brian asked me to run to get the water. He told me I had to go to the gym and fill the fifty-five-gallon garbage can. He seemed somber, and to my surprise, did not yell at me. *Oh man,* I thought to myself. *I can't even catch a break trying to deal with my ankle, lower back, and my wound. Jesus Christ, when will this end?*

Fortunately, my uncle decided to help me and show me where the water was. We got to the gym, where I found a garden hose attached to a spigot. I turned it on and filled the can while we sat in the truck bed. Once we returned to the tent, more crews began arriving from the other jobs. Somebody had fixed the regulator on the oil heating system, so we were finally getting heat inside the tent. However, when it comes to heating the inside of a tent, the process is quite different from heating a house, especially when the outside temperature is freezing. The only way to get warm was to stay about four to five feet away from the cover. Since there was not enough room for everything, we had to keep our cots right up against the freezing covering. So yeah, there was heat, but it was still cold as hell.

The weather conditions in the Iliamna area were unpredictable and extreme. It snowed, rained, iced up, and melted, and we had to contend with the ferocious, hazardous winds constantly. It was absolutely miserable.

Crew members were now flying in from the other villages, including Tim. I don't remember seeing Tim the night I got into my auto accident at Pitkas Point, so I am not sure if he was one of the coworkers who refused to take me to Bethel. He'd had four on his framing crew and one of them had to move on to another project, so now I was going to be his apprentice.

Even though he and Brian yelled at each other, I found Tim to be relatively quiet. But I had heard he had a temper. That's how some people cope in Alaska. You have to be tough as nails, and he was tough.

After breakfast, it was time to start working with the framing crew. By then, several floor systems, consisting of beams, floor joists, plywood, and soffits, had been completed, allowing us to start framing. The framing crew was responsible for building the exterior walls and installing the roof trusses. These were the identical houses that were built north of the Arctic Circle.

My biggest concern was meeting Tim's expectations. I didn't know if he knew about my injuries from the accident. I certainly did not tell him. If I didn't keep up, he might ride me fairly hard. I figured I should be as quiet as possible, not bug him with questions, and do exactly what I was told. Hopefully, that would compensate for my physical deficits on the job. We were fortunate that a forklift was on the job and could drop off the equipment and materials near the first house, so at least we wouldn't have to pack them to the site.

Each crew had its own specialized and standard equipment. They were provided with a small generator for power. At this time, we were using Yamaha generators, which were pretty damn good. Some would use Honda generators, which were also very good. We'd have to hand-carry all our tools to each site, including the gas cans and other equipment.

Our crew used a gas-fired, double-tank compressor to operate the nail guns. The compressors ran all day, and just like the generators, you'd have to fill them with gas, start them up, change the oils, maintain them, and so on. Even though it had a wheel on the front for rolling, I tell you, they were heavier and harder to drag around on top of the snowy, lumpy, frozen tundra than the generators. And you can guess who was charged with that task.

Tim was a man of action. I still had to run, not walk. I quickly learned Tim did not care about the working or the weather conditions. He did not tolerate the mention of problems or boneheaded mistakes; he would rip and tear down a person on the spot.

I was taught that a real man had to carry a minimum of six kiln-dried two-by-six studs, weighing about fifteen pounds each. That's about ninety pounds plus or minus, depending on how wet the lumber was.

Before my injuries, I could do such a task, but with my injuries, I couldn't pick up six; it was impossible. The most I could pick up was two, or three if I pushed myself. I struggled to carry them on my left shoulder because before my injuries, I had them on my dominant right shoulder. Fortunately, the left shoulder was not injured, so I made that work, but my lower back was still recovering, and I was still having problems with my right ankle.

I tried like hell to keep up with the crew all day, but I underperformed. To this day, I don't know why I wasn't fired because I did not carry the minimum of six studs. Maybe Tim knew of my injuries, but as far as I could tell from that day, he had no compassion for anyone. Perhaps he felt I was trying hard. Who knows?

The gable walls were the first to be built on each end of the house. Once that was framed, we attached the large premade gable truss to the top of the walls. This, in turn, would add anywhere from thirteen to fourteen feet to the height of the walls.

Once that was all nailed and clipped together, Tyvek, a synthetic weatherization barrier, was rolled out and stapled onto the studs and plates. When the Tyvek was secured, the siding was installed, covering the entire wall, including the gable trusses. We would then usually install the windows if available.

Naturally, each gable wall was very heavy to lift, somewhere around 1,200 pounds, and that did not include materials soaked with water or glazed over by ice. Depending on the time, Tim would make the very rare decision to leave the gable walls down, and we would have to come back the next morning to raise them. There were only four of us lifting these walls, and I could tell you it was heavy and dangerous work.

The working conditions were getting harsher. We were losing about five minutes of sunlight per day, and it was now October. We still had about ten hours of daylight, but we were heading into November. Darker, colder, windier, and rainier, all those elements would make our job much more trying.

Then things got unexpectedly worse. I don't know what happened, but the outhouse became unavailable, so we had to go outside. To make matters worse, the toilet paper had run out. Ok, that is fine if we were camping, but we were working. We had to scrounge around the job site to find what we could use for our needs. I would find a 16-penny nail box and use Tyvek or tar paper to clean myself, then throw it into the trash heap. I don't know what other people did, and I didn't ask.

Everybody was complaining, and we were all starting to get eccentric. That evening, I was told we needed to make the first house we built livable, install the roof, and insulate it so we could all use it as our crew campsite. The chef would still use the tent to cook from, but we would be inside the house as soon as possible.

The next morning, Tim sent me to help my uncle with the roof. It was blowing very hard.

"How are we going to lift each sheet of metal onto the roof?" I asked my uncle.

The metal sheets were approximately three feet wide and around eighteen feet long, depending on the size of the house. It's a lightweight material, but they are long and bulky, and they can also be very dangerous in high winds. If they are not adequately secured on the ground or the roof, the wind can blow them around like a kite in any direction, and they have the potential to severely injure a person by hitting them or slicing off their fingers, hands, or head.

My uncle explained that we would use three ladders on one side of the gable wall, place them about a foot above the roofline, and then tie them down. Two other people would be on the roof. They would throw ropes down the ladder side, and I would secure each rope to the c-vise grips, then clamp it to each end of the metal, ensuring they were secured enough not to come loose. That's precisely what we had done on the metal roof in Pitkas Point.

I did as he asked and slid the metal onto the ground near the gable walls myself. Once I had ensured my task was completed, he and his partner pulled the rope on each end, while I was at the bottom end of the middle ladder. I had to climb up the ladder holding the metal to ensure it was stable as they pulled it up, being very careful not to let go of the middle, as the wind could sometimes blow and catch it under the metal. I was so afraid that the wind would rip it out of my hands, causing it to fly up to the top of the roof and hurt my uncle or his partner.

Once we reached the top, we kept climbing and walked behind the sheet that had just been raised while my uncle and his partner slid the metal to the other end of the building, keeping it low to the purlins. Once they got it in place, they screwed it down. They didn't just set it. My uncle was wise; he always liked to screw each sheet off before installing another. That way, we did not have to come back and complete it.

Then, I scrambled back to the ladder, climbed down, and repeated the process until we were done with both sides. The last thing we had to do was install the ridge cap, which wasn't too bad because it was the very top of the roof with a six- to eight-inch opening. A person could walk along the ridge, placing their feet on the wooden trusses.

It was rapidly getting dark, and we were finally able to wrap up the job, having successfully installed the chimney flue. Everybody was happy, since that meant we were almost ready to move into the house. The crew teased me at dinner about how we had to get that thing insulated that night.

"Your dad wants it done," one of them said.

"Oh, you've got to be kidding me," I said.

"No, you need to go out there and insulate that house."

After dinner, I went back to the house. Somebody, probably the fork-lift operator, had already placed the bags of insulation inside the home. So, I started installing R-19 in the wall cavities by myself. The fact is that insulation is made from fiberglass. Fiberglass can get into your clothes, skin, eyes, and lungs. Fortunately, when I was about three-quarters of the way done with the walls, probably around midnight, my uncle came into the house to give me a hand with the rest of it. It was awfully kind of him.

Insulating the ceiling was a pain in the butt because, at that time, they didn't have blow-in insulation, or if they did, we didn't use it in the ceilings. We manually installed two pieces of insulation, R-38 and R-11, which increased the total R-factor in the ceilings to R-49. That is a lot of insulation, that's for sure. We finally finished around 3:00 a.m. I remember returning to the tent and lying on top of the ice-cold sleeping bag because I didn't want to get inside. I had no place to shower and was full of insulation. I didn't want to get fiberglass inside my sleeping bag, so I left my clothes on and just slept on top of the cot. What else could I do?

CHAPTER 17
No Holds Barred

Shortly after my stay in the hospital, I was still having difficulty turning my head from side to side. I saw many specialists back in Anchorage. Still in a cast a few weeks later, I began to have intermittent, sharp, needle-like pains in my left hand. I told my family and reported it to the doctor. It reminded me of getting shocked by the helicopter when I was a kid, but this was much more painful. No one said anything about the pain I was experiencing.

Shortly afterward, a person who was close to me drove me to an orthopedic specialist. I asked that person to leave the room, but to my surprise they refused. *I am here to make sure you get the right help.* Too weak to argue, I said nothing. When the doctor removed my cast, he noticed immediately that my hand would not come back to life. I could not move it. Staring at me with disbelief, he ran into the other room, rushed back, and put a neck brace on me.

"You need X-rays immediately," he announced.

A short time later, he put the X-rays on the light board and pointed to the image of my neck. I saw a horizontal crack in my neck vertebrae near where he was pointing.

"What is that?" I asked.

"I have bad news," he said. "You fractured your neck in the C4 and C5 area."

"I kept telling the Kamloops nurses and doctors that I had problems moving my head," I said. "They told me that my neck was OK because the X-rays from the trauma center had shown no injury to my neck. And because of that, they never put a neck brace on me."

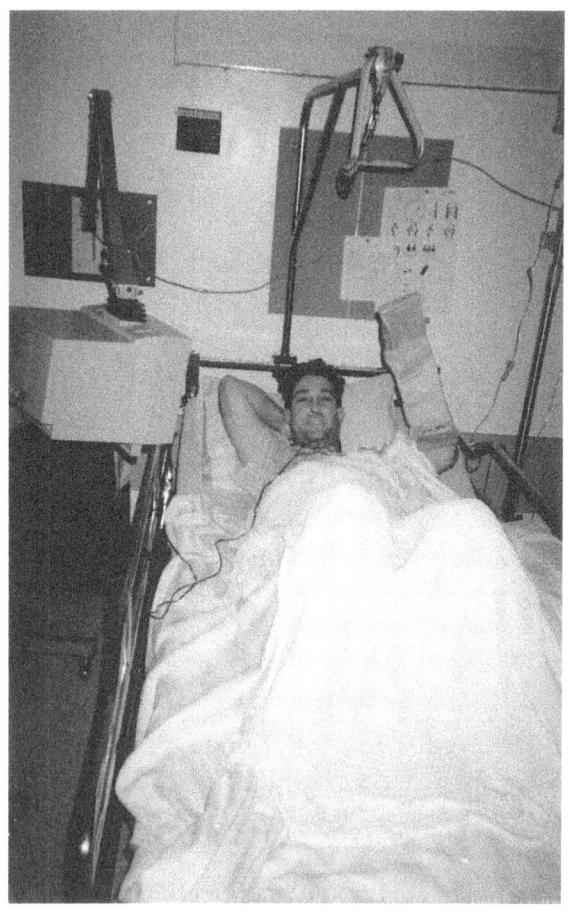

In bed in the Kamloops Hospital without a neck brace.

"I know, they missed it," the doctor said. "You're lucky not to be paralyzed."
Both of them left the room and I sat there by myself contemplating my
plight. I kept thinking, What now? How can this be? How is it that I am still
walking? The person I asked to leave walked back into my room by themselves,
gave me a hard look, and said, "You'd better tell the truth and not lie."

"What? Lie about what?"

"Your injuries."

"What the hell are you talking about? You can see my broken neck on
the X-rays, and the doctor said I fractured C4 and C5. Sick to my stomach
and with the little energy I had left, I shouted, "Get out, get out!" What the
hell was the matter with that person? I mean, the f**king X-ray was right
there in front of their face, clearly showing I broke my neck. And I'm asked
if I am faking my injuries. What kind of lowlife could have such hatred in
their heart? To this day, when I think about that time, I get so pissed off and
sick to my stomach. I couldn't even defend myself in my weakened condition.
What a f**king a** hole. As if I didn't have enough problems to deal with.

Finally, that person left. The doctor returned and, after a short discussion
about my neck, he looked at me with sympathetic eyes and told me, "Hang on,
don't give up. Go back to school and restart your life." He pointed out that thirty-
three was still relatively young. Then he reached into his pocket and pulled out
a folded white note, showing it to me. The doctor told me that the person who
drove me had handed him a note. It read, "Is David faking his injuries?"

"You're going to have a tough time recovering," he said. "Whoever is
behind that note won't make your recovery any easier."

After giving me a serious look, he whispered, "Do not talk to or trust
anyone. Take care of yourself and recover, change your life, and go to school
like I did." It turns out that he had worked in the trades. He, too, had life-
changing injuries and had to start all over again. He'd gone to college and
eventually became a doctor.

Having to deal with that nasty person, along with financial problems
and my ongoing injuries, was hard as hell, to say the least. I was grateful for

the advice the doctor gave me and told no one what was happening to me. I did not mention anything the doctor had said to me to that cruel person on the way home.

The intermittent sharp pain in my left hand continued to plague me for a couple more years. It was another specialist who discovered that one of the pins that was installed at the hospital had failed and was the cause of the pain. After I had the pin removed surgically, I never had that sharp pain again. They gave me the removed pin, which I still have as a reminder of the pain I went through.

THE NEXT MORNING, I woke up to the tent flapping loudly due to the wind. When I looked around the tent, I could see a lot of water on top of the plywood flooring. *This totally sucks,* I thought.

Once again, my clothes, which were underneath my cot, were soaking wet. After splashing through the water on the floor, I found a dry pair of socks in my duffel bag to put on. I had to keep my feet above the waterline to wear my socks. Luckily, my bunny boots were next to my bed. Once I got those on, I was able to make my way over to the kitchen and get a little sip of water before having to relieve myself outside, as we still had no operational outhouse.

I knew we were supposed to think, "It's no big deal. It's just camping." But it's not like we were there trying to live in the wilderness for a few days, rubbing two sticks together to make a campfire. Hell no, we weren't there to be weekend naturalists; we were there to work.

I kept trying to trick my mind that things weren't as bad as they were, even though I was still struggling with the wound in my shoulder and all the pain, but it just became grimmer as the days lost more and more light.

I knew that night we would be moving into the new house that we had just built and that my uncle and I had insulated, so at least it would be a lot warmer than staying in the tent. At the same time, we would be sleeping in a house full of uncovered insulation.

That's going to suck, I thought, *breathing all that fiberglass into our lungs.* We could have masked up if we had had masks, but we didn't have those or much in the way of safety equipment. It's just the way it was in those days.

It felt like a mini hurricane was going on outside, to say nothing of all that water and ice on the lumpy tundra where you could easily twist and break an ankle. *You've got to be kidding,* I thought. *Plus, we get to work out in this crap today. How fun.*

Even though the cook constantly complained that he couldn't get the type of food he wanted, the breakfast he served, which consisted of pancakes, eggs, and more, was always good, so starvation was the last thing I worried about. I was sick to my stomach, knowing that we had to go out into this weather and work for a boss who didn't care about what happened to us out there.

After breakfast, I made my way to the job site. Tim was usually the first person on the job, but at this point, it didn't matter because I thought he would change his mind and give us the day off. When arriving at the house, we realized that the entire floor was covered in about a quarter inch of ice and water lay on top of the ice. We could hardly stand on the deck without slipping and falling. All we had were regular snow boots, no cleats or spikes or anything like that, and we were to build on top of this deck that day. How were we going to do that?

As usual, Tim shouted, "Get to work, f**kers." I think he was born with that hashtag in his mouth.

What distressed me the most was that the siding was placed far away from the house. I had to carry or slide the damn pieces to the houses. What made it more challenging was the ice buildup. It made the nine-foot-long, fifty-eight-pound sheets much heavier. I used my hammer to try to chip off as much ice as I could, but that turned out to be a complete waste of time and energy. I couldn't hit too hard because I didn't want to damage the finished surface, which would make the sheets unusable.

At first, I tried to drag the siding on the tundra to the house, but it was too difficult for me to move. I then tried to carry the sheets on my shoulder, but the wind was blowing so hard that the air pressure kept twisting my back side to side. The only way I could carry it was on my right shoulder, on top of the open wound. Not only was it painful, but I could also hear the bandage crackling and rubbing against me. *This totally sucked.* I was just sick about it, but who would I complain to? Who was I going to ask for help? Tim kept screaming louder and louder as the wind continued to blow harder. "Work, f**kers, work! Come on, get that wood up here," he screamed while thumping away with his nail gun, nailing everything together.

Eventually, we pushed the gable trusses onto the deck and attached them to the walls. The windows were left out due to the high winds. We placed blocks underneath the gable trusses, allowing us to lift the walls from underneath. Tim reminded us that the gable trusses had nails protruding through the boards. *Yeah, he's right, so we need to be careful.* We were now ready to lift both gable walls.

Tim assigned our positions to lift the wall. He and Levi, a carpenter, were to lift each end of the wall, which was the lowest and safest area as they were right on the edge of the building, allowing them to jump out of the way in case the wall fell back toward them. Benny, the other crewmember, and I were assigned to lift the middle, which was the heaviest, highest, and most dangerous part of the wall to lift. The sheer height of the wall would make it extremely difficult to escape if it collapsed onto us, especially with slippery ice covering the entire floor.

The strong wind continued to blow directly toward us. Tim yelled, "Lift, f**kers, lift, come on, f**king lift!" as we slipped around on the ice, struggling to raise it to knee height. The wind kept pressing the gable back down, sliding us backwards every time we took a tiny step forward.

"F**kers, lift! Lift the f**king wall! Come on, a**holes, lift!" he kept shouting. Finally, after what felt like an eternity, but was probably around thirty seconds, we got it up to our hips.

"OK," he yelled. "This is it. Keep going!"

We started lifting again, getting it just past our hips before it began to slide back below our hips again. We took another step and got it up to our ribs, but again, we kept sliding backward.

As Tim repeatedly screamed at us to keep lifting, we finally managed to lift it just above our heads. Still fighting the wind and the ice, we managed to get it up. God only knows how we finally got the damn thing vertical. By then, I was shaking like crazy. The gable was way above my head. I'm only five foot ten, and that wall was over thirteen feet tall. That was a pretty damn tall wall and heavy as hell.

"Get a brace! Get a f**king brace, f**ker, brace!" Tim continued to scream at me.

I was afraid to let go of the wall because I feared that the guys would lose control. I quickly flipped around, tried to sprint to get a brace, and immediately slipped and fell on my hands and knees. I tried to get up, but the icy floor prevented me from standing, so I crawled as fast as I could to get out of the way of the wall and grab a brace.

As I grabbed a brace, I was able to stand up. As I turned around, I could see the guys still holding the wall, but they were slowly sliding backwards. Tim and Levi jumped off the edge of the building to avoid being hit by the wall. Poor Benny tried to get out of the way, but he was not quick enough. The top part of the gable truss slammed into Benny's right shoulder, leaving him with substantial puncture marks from the nails protruding, and Levi injured his ankle jumping off the side of the building. Tim and I escaped without a scratch.

With no compassion or mercy toward the poor guys who got injured, Tim angrily said, "You f**kers, should have held your ground."

Tim was hell bent on raising both gable walls. He immediately re-
cruited the flooring crew to assist us in raising them. I felt bad for my injured coworkers because our only break from the incident was waiting for
help to arrive. It took ten people to raise the walls. With the walls finally
up and braced off, we built the rest of the house.

Later that night, we slept inside the house we had insulated from the
night before. They used a kerosene oil space heater for warmth. Fortunately, kerosene is much cleaner than diesel oil, but we still had to inhale
all those fumes. Still, it was better than freezing, vastly warmer, and better
than the tent, no doubt about it.

The next day, I woke up to a cold, sunny morning after my first warm
night's rest. Even though we still were without an outhouse and shower, I
felt better about our living conditions. While heading to breakfast in the
tent, now called the cook shack, I noticed blood had soaked from my
shoulder to the outside of my jacket. After breakfast, I looked at the walls
I had worked on the day before and saw blood smudged on several of the
siding pieces that I'd carried over. The whole damn thing discussed me.

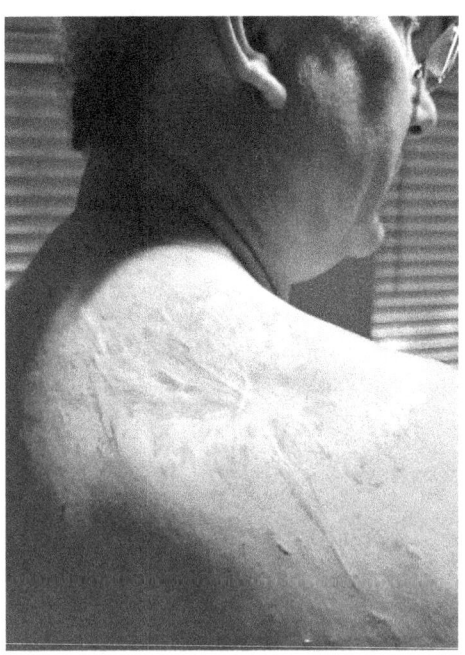

Staring out, watching the sunrise, I pondered what kind of idiot I was working in these conditions. I was so lonely, angry, and bitter that I had no one to talk to. What was I to do? My coworkers were dealing with similar working conditions, but none of them had been working for so long with severe injuries as I had. Fear was the glue that kept me going, and I didn't want to fail and let people down. I believed I was helping those I respected and loved.

I wasn't the only unhappy person. The harsh working conditions began to erode our normal personalities, and before long, I noticed us morphing into new characters to cope with our reality.

People teased each other, saying many stupid, immature, and inappropriate things. I can tell you it was getting crazy. We developed a sick type of humor to cope with the bizarre behavior people were exhibiting, including my own. Even when someone humorously told a shocking story, it didn't conceal the fact that people were capable of doing terrible things. To this day, there are many things I have not told a soul. The trail of thoughts I am now sharing is just pieces of a large puzzle that will remain incomplete because it is too painful to discuss.

Years later, in college, my psychology professor had us watch and discuss the film version of the "Stanford Prison Experiment." I learned that when a group of people works closely together, especially in stressful situations, they can develop aggressive and inappropriate behavior patterns that contradict their core values, causing them to do and say things they would usually never do outside that environment. "The experiment, which was scheduled to last 1-2 weeks, ultimately had to be terminated on the 6th day as the experiment escalated out of control when the prisoners were forced to endure cruel and dehumanizing abuse at the hands of their peers.

The experiment showed, in Dr. Zimbardo's words, how 'ordinary college students could do terrible things.'"[5]

The lesson gave me another tool to help me understand what was happening to all of us. I mean, they had to stop the psychology experiment on

day six in a controlled environment. Can you imagine how some of us be-
haved while living in the bush for weeks or months at a time? What about
a child being exposed to similar circumstances? I thought it was just me
who was having problems adjusting to polite society. Suddenly, I was not
alone. Even with that information, I still found it hard to adjust to life
back home.

By this time, we had erected many houses resembling a subdivision.
After dinner, I would at times help other crew members. One night, I
helped Yukon get some plumbing parts. Laughing, he asked, "Want to see
how I locate the chimney flues?" He then unzipped his thick winter cov-
eralls and pulled out a concealed pistol. As he walked to the furnace, he
reached up, pointing the pistol to the ceiling, and shot through the roof. I
couldn't believe it. I thought the biker plumber would have done something like that, not Yukon. I thought he was a pacifist and disliked guns.
Who knows where that bullet went? What if someone was on the roof?
The madness was escalating.

The next day, I noticed dogs running throughout the job site while I
was nailing the top plate to the studs. I heard the familiar sound of gun-
shots. Not the thumping of a nail gun, but rifle shots. Some guys were
shouting, "Get him, get him! He's getting away, he's getting away!" *Oh,
just great, now what? Not again. F**k me.* Crack—another shot—then a
couple more shots rang out, followed by whimpering and high-pitched
screeching that sounded like it came from a dog.

I didn't know what the hell was going on. As I looked to the left of me,
I could see a dog dragging its hind legs and whimpering as two guys with
rifles ran in between the houses, chasing and shooting at the dog.

"I'll get this one," one of the men shouted as they ran past us. "Get the
other dog."

More shots rang out then, and the moaning dog was silenced. Our
crew and others looked around, trying to assess the situation. Then, we
went right back to work, ignoring what had just happened.

That night, many crew members were laughing about the day's events.

"What the hell is going on?" I asked one of my coworkers. "Why are they shooting dogs?"

"The city put a bounty on the dogs."

"Why?"

He told me that many dogs become rabid, and they are a danger to the locals, especially the children. I didn't know that people actually shot dogs. I thought that was in the movies. I had no idea this was something that still occurred in modern times. I love dogs, but I had to put the incident in the back of my mind, so I twisted my compassionate thoughts about the dogs getting slaughtered into a simple statement: So long as they don't hit me with their bullets. I had little to no empathy toward the dogs. How pathetic.

What can you do, either cry or laugh? From my point of view, it was more of a cry where the pain cuts so deep I can't make heads or tails of it. What was going on with this job? Everyone was dealing with the weather, injuries, and lack of bathroom and bathing facilities, and watching this was just another day's work.

The next morning, we crawled out of bed and got to work. Tim hired another worker, an elderly guy well-known in the local community. I will call him Jeff. Though he had been looking for a job swinging a hammer, Tim told him there wasn't much he could do at that time besides trash pickup. He told him that he would be able to frame in about a week.

Jeff accepted his offer, and Tim instructed him to meet with the fork-lift operator to begin work immediately. Jeff said he would be back on Monday.

"We have work for you right now," he responded.

"Yes, I know, but since it's Wednesday, I don't want a small check, so I need to start on Monday so my checks are the same," Jeff said.

"What? You'll make more money starting today," Tim said. Jeff left the site, and we didn't see him for the rest of the week.

Monday rolled around. That afternoon, I saw a man in the distance walking toward our job site. Still not recognizing his face as he got closer, I saw him holding a box out at arm's length. *What a strange sight, I thought.* I went back to work. Jeff headed toward our site and shouted at Tim. "Hey, there's s**t in these boxes! There's f**king s**t in these boxes." He set the box on the floor and opened it up to show Tim that there was crap in it. "I was hired to be a carpenter, not a s**t mover," he shouted.

Who could blame him? I would have been pissed off, too.

Tim just stared at Jeff. "I got nothing else for you. What do you want me to do? You'll be framing soon, but this is all I got for you right now."

Jeff threw the box down and stomped off, shaking his head in disgust. During lunch, people talked about the box and what Jeff had done. We felt bad for the guy. No one was trying to disrespect him or the local community. We were all pissed off because we were trying to solve a difficult problem with the lack of bathroom facilities. I mean, what were we supposed to do? Besides, who opens boxes headed for the dump?

After the fiasco with Jeff, it wasn't long before we were informed that the tribal council had decided to shut us down because we were not allowed to sleep in the houses we were building, and we had to have a functioning outhouse on the jobsite. "The buyers won't purchase these houses if you occupy them," we were told. "You all have to move back to the tent."

Shortly after that, we suddenly had bathroom facilities on the job site. However, we still didn't have showers. I don't really remember taking showers. I knew I smelled bad; that was a given, but that was the least of my problems. Now we had to move back into the freezing tent.

Over the next few weeks, we experienced heavy winds, snow, rain, and everything else Mother Nature had to offer. My nineteenth birthday came and went without a mention, and it was almost Thanksgiving.

I knew that within a couple of days, we would have a company Thanksgiving dinner at the Iliamna Lodge, and my family would be there.

In the meantime, we were now down to just seven and a half hours of daylight. During the winter, we usually worked long hours in the freezing darkness of night. I'd wear a face mask and at times it was so cold that every time I exhaled, the steam from my mouth would hit my eyes, and when I'd blink, my eyelashes would freeze together. The only way I could open my eyelids outside was to keep pressing my exposed fingertips onto my eyelids and melt the ice.

We had to think outside the box to keep the equipment and under-powered generators running. We even worked by flashlight if the generators ran out of fuel or broke down. One time, a crew ran out of motor oil that lubricates the generators and equipment; a person from that crew took vegetable oil from the cook shack, poured it into their generator, and ran it all day. I couldn't believe it worked. None of the equipment was designed to run on vegetable oil, so I don't know if that generator eventually blew up.

Just before Thanksgiving, the wind howled like a hurricane, blowing our materials and trash everywhere. My uncle and I, along with many others, had to secure our materials and attempt to move as much waste as possible to a safe location. What we couldn't move, we tried to secure it with big sheets of plywood. It was rough going being pelted by rain, snow, and sleet. I kept asking my dad for help and wondering why I was still alive and he was dead.

After lunch, we went to one of the houses to secure loose metal roofing. My uncle and I were assigned to fix a sheet flapping in the high wind. As I approached, an 18-foot sheet came flying toward me. I tried to dodge, raised my left arm to shield my head, and the metal wrapped around my body, folded in half, then flew over me. I chased it down, pinned it, and my uncle came to help. The sheet was crumpled from hitting me, but somehow, I wasn't cut or hurt. I couldn't believe I walked away unharmed.

After securing the rest of the metal, I returned to the large forklift we used for trash. We built a box and set it on the front forks. Jeff was now operating the forklift, and he followed me around while I picked up trash and put it in the box.

I never liked working around Jeff. Just being in his presence was unsettling. Other crew members were equally uncomfortable around him or downright afraid of him. I had heard many rumors about Jeff from locals in and out of the village. Allegedly, he and his girlfriend were drunk one night in the middle of winter while driving back from Nondalton to Newhalen on a four-wheeler. They got into a fight with his wife, and Jeff flew into a drunken rampage. And, well, the next day someone found a badly bruised, bloody, naked body lying on the frozen trail. A woman had been run over by a four-wheeler so many times that they could not identify the body until they brought it back to Iliamna. The victim was Jeff's wife, and the alleged murderer turned out to be Jeff. Whether or not he was guilty, I felt creepy working around that man. I'm not saying he did it, but I wanted to avoid him as much as possible.

More disturbing, we built Jeff's girlfriend's house. I never liked that lady, even before I knew about what had happened. She was hard and seemed wicked, and I never wanted to engage with her. The only thing I did was say hello and get as far away from her as fast as I could because her tone and attitude creeped me out. Additionally, my boss employed her. Her job was anyone's guess.

Finally, we got the news that the crew was moving to the following job site in Nondalton. What a relief! This would be the final set of homes, so there was light at the end of the tunnel. Once finished, we would be able to go home. Plus, we would no longer have to stay in a freezing tent as they'd rented a hall with showers and bathrooms.

At least I'll be able to clean my wound and try to get some relief somehow and recover in that village, I thought. Little did I know what was in store for me.

CHAPTER 18
Nondalton

As time went by after my disconcerting doctor visit, a friend and I went to see Lost in Space. *Still significantly tired due to my injuries and stress, I figured watching the movie and being with my dear friend would take my mind off things for a moment.*

I didn't say much when he picked me up. I couldn't summon the energy. About a quarter of the way into the movie, I felt like I was slipping away. For the first time since the two auto accidents I had been in, I again felt like I was dying. I couldn't talk.

"Are you OK?" my friend asked.

When I didn't answer, he repeatedly asked, getting louder.

I couldn't speak or move. I was upset that I couldn't answer my friend and felt bad for scaring him, but I felt frozen.

He rushed me to the hospital, and I still could not talk. One of my family members arrived at the hospital.

"There's nothing wrong with him," I heard the doctors tell them. "He is just not answering." Shortly after that, my ability to talk returned, but the experience haunted me for years.

I realized that I had finally gone into shock that night. My mind and body had shut down because of all the things I had gone through. Not only was I dealing with the insurance companies and finding all the financial difficulties overwhelming, but it looked like I was going to lose my houses, businesses, and livelihood as a carpenter.

All of this was because I was doing a favor to help my stepfather. The truck driver who hit me with what turned out to be a commercial double-trailer truck had jackknifed into my lane, going fifty-five miles an hour. I was going thirty-five, which is a ninety-mile-an-hour impact.

ON THE VERY short flight to Nondalton, which is nestled between mountains on both sides, I noticed there was much more snow on the ground than in Newhalen. That wasn't the only difference. The village had many trees and a single road that led straight to the airport on the town's edge. As we approached the midpoint of the town, I saw from the air that someone had already started some of the foundation pads I'd helped install previously. I also noticed completed floor systems. However, something seemed a little strange to me. These floor systems seemed to be higher above the ground. It was not a flat area like Newhalen or most of the other locations we built north of the Arctic Circle. This was different.

We landed. Brian's brother drove up, pulling a trailer in an orange-reddish Kubota tractor. He smiled and looked like a "Farmer Joe," which made me giggle. He was such a nice guy; it was always a pleasure to see him. I don't know how he managed to maintain his high spirits, but he always seemed happy and in a good mood.

Whenever I saw him, I would think about his lifelong dream of being a commercial fisherperson. Maybe that's what sustained him—because he would always say he was one more dollar closer to reaching his dream.

We unloaded the plane and loaded everything into the back of the trailer, then fired up the Kubota's diesel engine. While on our way to the crew house, we drove through town, and I could see that my assessment was correct about the height of the floor systems—they were much higher than we'd ever built. They were built on a steep hillside that rose from a flat parallel road. Some of these houses were so high in the air that you could stand underneath the base platforms and need a ladder to reach the first floor.

Most of the houses' foundations were incomplete in a way I'd never seen before. I found out later that they had to weld extensions on diagonal metal brackets, which had been ordered from a manufacturer, so we would have to wait to build those houses. In the meantime, vertical poles supported the entire system, and much of the metal lateral bracing was missing on many floors, creating a particularly hazardous situation. I imagined that as we began to build on an unstable foundation, the weight of the materials and the workers' movements could twist the vertical upright poles, start to twist the flooring, and cause the house to collapse to the ground, injuring or killing workers.

They had some temporary two-by-fours connecting tie-downs for that lateral bracing, but that looked sketchy. I noticed that thick ice had built up everywhere, and the foundation pads appeared to have shifted down the slope.

We turned up the road halfway through town and found ourselves at the camp. It was an old building that resembled a community center. The kitchen was in the back, along with tables, chairs, and several cots surrounding them. This place was vastly nicer and warmer than our previous camp. And to my great relief, there was running water and bathroom facilities. *Holy cow, now we have some comforts of civilization.* We were asked to select cots and store our belongings underneath them. The next thing I knew, I was out working. I hadn't even brushed my teeth, so that would have to wait.

I had to help Brian's brother move materials with the Kubota. He had been moving 500-pound boilers by himself. I don't know how the hell he did it, but somehow he had gotten them into and out of the trailer by himself. He was built like an ox and was the nicest guy to work with. We continued moving materials for days until the other crews came over. We lugged the materials up the side of the hill and onto the lower parts of the deck, which were about three feet high, while the higher elevated side was around eight to nine feet off the ground. We worked long into every night.

Now we were able to shower, but my uncle, out of the kindness of his heart, was still bandaging my shoulder. I was still in a lot of pain from my injuries, but I was starting to feel better, at least physically. I continued to have flashbacks of the accident and of sliding down the gravel road. I could hear the truck crunching and rolling down the road, and see the headlights flashing in my mind. My mind was still trying to process the accident.

The weather was dreadful. It was snowing, cold, and seriously uncomfortable. Many people were quitting right and left. Nobody wanted to work on this isolated project in the middle of winter, surrounded by ice, snow, and wind. The situation became so dire that my stepfather had to place an ad in multiple newspapers to recruit the workforce, including some from the lower 48. Every time someone flew in, they wouldn't last.

On the Newhalen job, I remember these two guys arrived late in the afternoon to build the interior walls, which meant they didn't have to work outside. The next morning, one of the guys got up, looked around, and said, "We quit." The two went directly to the airport and paid their own way back.

We were obviously behind schedule, and the roofs were not getting done. My poor uncle was working his ass off and doing everything he could to get the houses closed in. I helped him whenever I could, between my other jobs.

Late one evening, after we finally stopped work and returned to camp to eat dinner, I saw my brother-in-law and Gil, whom I had known since I was a small kid working in Kotzebue. I don't know how old he was, but he looked like a happy grandpa even when I first met him. All these years later, he looked as if he hadn't aged one bit. I had always liked him. He was a very nice guy and always kind to me. Now he was here, and I couldn't believe it.

It turned out that they had flown in from town that day to give us a hand. I didn't even know that Gil was still working because the last time I had heard was that his poor daughter had died. My understanding was that while she was driving a snow machine, she ran into a wire fence that struck her hand and head. Well, I won't say anymore. My heart started to beat fast as I realized that maybe that coffin that my uncle and I put in my stepfather's 402 twin-engine aircraft might have been her. I felt so bad. In any case, it was a devastating blow that she had passed away. *God rest her soul.*

I don't know how he was able to handle such an enormous loss. He was a brave, compassionate person, the type who would give the shirt off his back if someone needed help. When I heard what happened to his daughter, even though I do not remember meeting her, I felt heartbroken. Yet, here he was, still the same smiley, happy guy. I was so glad to have the opportunity to see him again.

"What are you doing here?" I asked my brother-in-law.

"Your father asked me to help," he replied. "How's your shoulder?"

I told him it was still bleeding, but not as much, and that it was oozing a lot of pus, and I was still taking gravel out, something I continue to have to do now when small chunks eventually work their way through the scar tissue. It was a real pain. "At least I'm finally capable of cleaning it myself," I told him. "But it's still hard to put on a bandage by myself."

I added that at least we were finally in a warm building, and he responded that he'd heard we were having lots of difficulties. After a good meal and a night's sleep, we woke up early the next day and started working.

My brother-in-law jumped in to help my uncle on the roof. The good thing was that he was a competent construction worker who was a superintendent for a small contractor. He could do it all, concrete, frame, drywall, and finish work. I always enjoyed working for him.

He was always so kind and pleasant. I had a lot of respect for him and still do to this day.

As we moved the materials down the road, I saw them working hard on the roofs. By then, a few of the houses had roofs on, and the job was starting to come together, even though we were still struggling with a lack of human power. We made great efforts to do what we could by working late in the evening. I don't know about anyone else, but I didn't charge for many of my overtime hours. I think some other folks did that as well.

One Friday night, the crew was having dinner and chatting with Gil and some locals about Kotzebue, where he was from. Many people were drinking. I don't remember if I was or not. I must have had something, but for the first time, I could relax and enjoy everyone's company. Everyone else seemed to be having a good time as well.

"Hey, you're from f**king Kotzebue?" asked one of the locals.

Gil laughed loudly while drinking his whiskey. "Yeah, I'm from f**king Kotzebue," he said.

The locals started giving Gil a bunch of s**t. The bantering went back and forth for quite some time as they took turns ripping each other. I had heard the history of the big Native wars. It wasn't until that moment that I realized there was still anger and resentment within some Native communities that were carried forward to the present day. The taunting was relentless. Both the locals and Gil were laughing their butts off as they teased each other, and everybody seemed to go to bed happy.

The next day, I had to help my brother-in-law and uncle work on the roofs. We didn't exactly take weekends off. This house was high up on the hill. A couple of days prior, my boss's brother had moved some materials to the home. We stored the smaller items underneath the house to protect them from the elements, but the bigger items, such as the refrigerator and the boiler, were placed about five feet in front of the house.

I was handing up material and whatnot to them as they were up on the roof screwing it down. It was snowing, so everyone was slipping and sliding everywhere. Some metal had not been screwed off from the day before, so my brother-in-law went out there holding a screw gun with the electrical cord. I knew a rope was nearby, but the next thing I knew, he was sliding down the roof.

"Hang on!" I shouted. "Hang on, please hang on!"

Somehow, just before falling off the roof's edge, he did the impossible: he flipped himself around during his rapid descent on a snowy, icy roof. Now, face forward, he was riding on all fours, and as he was about to go over the edge, he jumped out of our sight. He had fallen at least sixteen to seventeen feet from the top edge of the snowy roof and onto an icy, snowy, frozen slope.

Oh my God, Jesus Christ!

We were freaked out. *My God, I hope he's OK.*

"Are you OK?" we yelled as we climbed off the roof.

He was. He had hurt his hands, feet, and back, but it could have been much worse. If he hadn't jumped, he would have landed on top of any of the objects below, potentially severely injuring his spinal cord, breaking bones, or impaling himself. His quick agility set him on a course that landed him between the refrigerator and the boiler. He survived by the skin of his teeth. Due to his remarkable bravery, courage, and quick thinking, he saved his own life and prevented a significant injury.

Oh, Christ Almighty, thank God he's not seriously hurt, I thought.

He returned to the roof and kept working even though it was still snowing. He was just a trooper. I only knew of the injuries he told us about, but given the height of the fall, I am sure there were more.

My brother-in-law could have been crippled for life or died. Shaken up, I kept thinking, *God, what the hell are we doing? Nobody wants to work out here. I loved that man and my uncle. If either one of them had gotten hurt or died, I think I would have lost my mind.*

A couple of days later, we returned to the camp to rest and found that the locals had demolished our stuff. They went inside the camp, stole lots of people's stuff, and trashed the place, smashing up the tables, chairs, and cots. It was like they took a sledgehammer to the place. The cooking facilities were broken and messy.

That evening, we had to leave the camp and find one of the houses that had already been insulated. It was unpleasant because the houses had no heat or electricity. At least windows had been installed in the one we chose, but one was broken. So, it was freezing cold. The cots were destroyed, we had no mats to sleep on, and the floor was freezing cold. I laid my sleeping bag on the insulation and used that for padding.

The next thing I knew, more people were quitting. My brother-in-law left the job. My uncle stayed on the job, but not on the premises. I don't remember where he went, probably to another village. I was out there with just a couple of people, feeling abandoned, isolated, and scared for my safety.

I contacted my stepfather. "I don't want to stay here unless we have some Doberman pinschers, or some sort of guns, or something like that for protection," I told him.

"Hang on," he said. "We got another guy coming out there to help straighten things out."

"The last time I saw Brian was weeks ago," I said, unable to hide my emotion. "I've rarely seen him because he is always flying around to all the other villages running the project. What do you mean you're getting another person?"

"I hired a new project manager who'll be flying out today or tomorrow. We are going to get some help soon," he said.

I held my tongue because I didn't want to cause any more problems. I returned to the cold, unheated house and fell asleep on my sleeping bag, still using the insulation as a mat since there were no cots.

The next day, those who stayed had to deal with the new reality of the days ahead. There were no longer any bathroom facilities, and no kitchen was available. All we had to eat was some canned food that we had grabbed the day before from the old camp. When we went to retrieve some of our belongings from the old camp, we found that the door was locked, and we were denied entry, so we were unable to salvage anything else.

From what I had heard, the new boss was flying out in his airplane, a Helio Courier aircraft. These famous planes had been used in Vietnam and were supposedly designed to avoid stalling. I never bought that for one second, because all aircraft can stall. Later that afternoon, I heard a plane flying overhead. From hanging around airports and runways, I automatically knew it was a Helio aircraft just by the sound. Looking up confirmed that.

Oh, that must be the new boss, already. Holy cow, he is coming to help us out. That would be great.

We met him at the house where we were staying. He had curly hair and resembled Tom Jones, the entertainer. We told him what had happened.

"I'm going to make things right without delay and work out a deal so we can use the base camp again," he said. He seemed like a reasonably nice guy who wanted to help us. Shortly after that meeting, he took off and flew to Iliamna. I guess he was going to check out the other jobs.

That same day, before he ever had a chance to renegotiate deals with the locals and get us back into the camp, let alone deal with the destruction of our property, news arrived. While taking off on the taxiway at Iliamna Airport, he crashed. So much for the legend that those planes don't stall. We were told it was a terrible crash and that he was being medevacked to Anchorage. I hoped he was OK. Jesus, the poor guy wasn't even out here for a few hours, and he crashed. *What more could go wrong with this job?*

Many weeks later, I would see the new supervisor at his home. He was banged up and had casts on both legs and feet. Wires were sticking out of every toe. His face was black and blue. He didn't look well at all, but he was able to talk on the phone for hours.

More people working in the other villages had quit after the new project manager crashed, and a few familiar workers arrived in Nondalton. We were pretty much by ourselves. It was so cold by that point that the Kubota wouldn't start very well. The fuel filter line would crystallize with ice, and we had to use space heaters to get it to start.

In addition to all my other duties, I helped Yukon and the biker plumber. This time, the plumbers needed water and glycol to be injected into the boiler systems to activate the heating system. All we had was a hose from the sink inside the cook camp to fill up five-gallon buckets. Once filled, we intended to use the Kubota trailer and drive it to each home. However, as luck would have it, the Kubota's fuel line froze up again, and we could not get power to a space heater to melt the ice. So now, everything had to be moved by hand.

Because Yukon wanted to go home ASAP, it was decided that we'd do a twenty-four-hour work marathon. Just my luck, I had to hand-carry the five-gallon buckets of water back and forth from one end of the village to the other in subzero temperatures all through the night and the next day. Each bucket weighed over thirty-five pounds when filled with water. The road had a light layer of snow covering the ice below. At times, my boots would hit an open patch of ice, and I would slip and splash icy water on my face or exposed skin, causing a burning sensation. After reaching a house, I'd carry the buckets of water up the stairs and pump the water and glycol mixture into each boiler. Glycol is an antifreeze product that keeps water from freezing in subzero conditions. We finished that twenty-four-hour shift and completed the job. Yukon was tired, but happy because now he could go home.

The hits kept coming, but I was able to make lemonade out of lemons. I would wind up striking out on my own. At the age of nineteen, I bought a cute, small, two-bedroom condominium located on the second floor. It had a shared garage, which was nice, especially during the dark, cold winter days in Anchorage. I had a few good years there and eventually sold it, moving on to other adventures and applying the lessons I had learned.

CHAPTER 19
Everlasting Lessons

During the trial, a big, burly person with a beard and mustache testified that he had come up to the crumpled truck and seen me unconscious. He saw my left-hand dangling outside the front driver's-side window. As I sat in the mangled truck, the man tried to wake me up by talking to me, but I didn't respond even after he shook me. Out of desperation, he smacked my left hand hard a couple of times, but still I remained unconscious.

As he told the story on the witness stand, he started to break down and cry. He had heard that my left hand had to be reconstructed with pins.

I watched him cry on the stand. God, I felt so bad for him. He had not known my hand was damaged after being blown through the window, shattering the glass. It was not his fault. If I saw someone in trouble in a similar incident, I might have done the same thing he did. There was nothing for him to be upset about. I know he was there trying to help me.

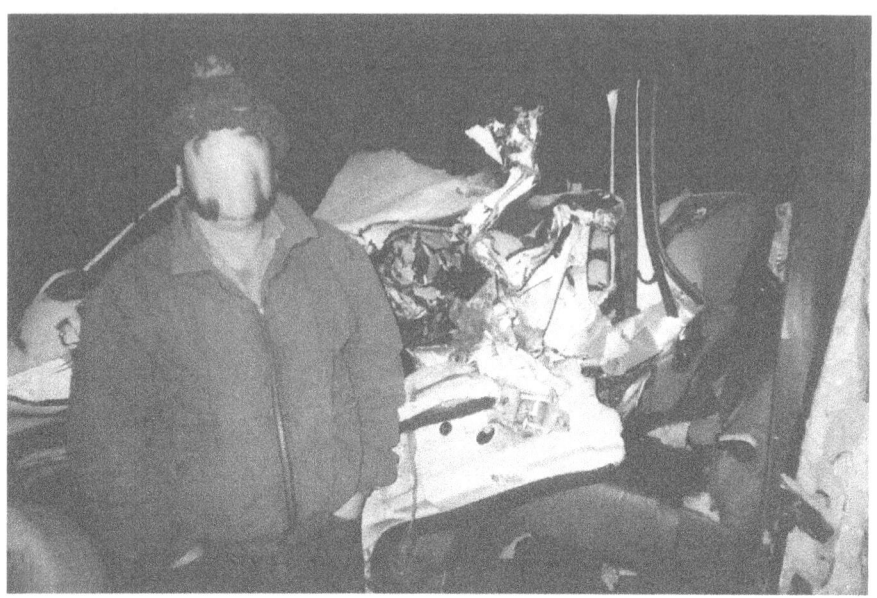

I don't hold any hard feelings against the truck driver who hit me. However, I am disgusted with the despicable insurance companies that left me financially stranded and couldn't have cared less about my or others' well-being as they fought over money.

The financial hardships and injuries I had to deal with shook me to the core. And even more disgusting was that for several years, the hospital denied our request for the X-ray of my neck from the trauma center. Finally, just before or during the trial, the hospital released the X-ray. It showed that I had damaged my C4 and C5 vertebrae. They had kept that under wraps. They just said, "Sorry that we made a mistake," and that was it.

Financially, they treated my neck injury no differently than someone breaking a finger. It was no issue for them. Imagine yourself trying to deal with all that. I could have been paralyzed if my left hand had not come back to life and my doctor had immediately suspected something was wrong—pure luck. My doctor saved me from being in a wheelchair, and no one was held accountable.

I had a tough time trying to recover from that accident, and of course, I had to pay for my medical bills for years, which cost me my home, job, and business rental homes. I received little to no help from my family.

Luckily, by then, I had created my own family based on love.

AFTER WE RETURNED from Newhalen and Nondalton, my stepfather told me he held no grudges against anyone who'd quit and would hire them back if they wanted a job. Even though I remained loyal and didn't quit, I was treated much differently from all the other workers. Things were never the same between us. We never discussed my auto accident and the hardships I'd endured in the villages. It was a dead subject, even though to this day I continue to struggle with what had happened on those jobs, along with the acts of violence I'd had to deal with as a child.

While recovering from my second auto accident down in Mexico, I had a strong urge to find my biological father's burial site. I felt the need to tell him I loved him and to apologize for harming him. Once I was healed enough, I headed to Los Angeles to search for his grave. It took some time, but I finally found him. A logbook had to be signed before going to the site. Strangely, I saw a signed name above my signature. Who was that person? As I approached his grave, I noticed a small, beautiful plaque. After I visited with him, I returned to the office and asked the caretaker about the signature.

"That person purchased the plaque," he said.

At that moment, I realized who that was. I had always been told I had another brother who was older than me. I don't know how much older he was, but I was told his name, and they emphasized that he was absolutely gorgeous. Stunning, movie star looks. I was also told he was very protective of my stepsister, as well as other people, and that he would look after her like a hawk. Unfortunately, I have no memory of him. I only remember my beautiful little two-year-old brother. But I was touched that our older brother had had a plaque engraved for our father.

Oh, my precious brother, thank you so much for the love you have shown to Dad, I thought. *God bless my brother, both my brothers.*

Even though I felt a little better after visiting my father, I still suffered from tremendous guilt. I know it made no logical sense that a four-year-old boy who loved his father could have killed him. Of course, that made no sense. I knew that, but my mind would not release me from that burden.

It was time to leave Los Angeles, but something kept gnawing at me. And that was how my father died. So, I decided to work up enough courage to ask my biological mom, with whom I'd gotten back in touch, about what had happened to him.

When I explained to her over the phone what I had been told, she started to cry.

"That's not what happened," she insisted before explaining that he had been on his motorcycle at a gas station and that a car ran him over and took off. "A hit and run," she said. "They did not find the person who killed your father. The case is still open."

"No, that's not true. That can't be,"

"I have always known my first name was Lee before they changed it to David, but what I learned is that my father's middle name was Lee," I told her.

"It was as if someone was trying to erase his history," she said. She was depressed and angry about that for years.

After our conversation, I immediately called my grandmother, who was fortunately still alive at the time, and asked her the same question. Without hesitation, she told me the same story.

Grandmother tried to calm me down, but the pain of what I had just been told was indescribable. *God rest her soul.*

I cried and cried for a long time. *Why would someone tell me that he killed himself and have me believe that I'd killed him?* Not only was I lied to about how he died, but I learned that he'd just turned thirty-two years old. Was he in pain? Did he suffer while lying on the hot asphalt? *Dear God in heaven, I hope he did not suffer.*

Then rage came over me. What kind of person tells a child such a lie? A family member once claimed it was all a misunderstanding. Bulls**t. There's no way anyone could misinterpret something like that. But fine, let's give the benefit of the doubt. Even so, who in their right mind would say something like that to a seven-year-old? That's when it hit me: I've been grieving all along.

For years, I've reflected on the pain caused by that person's relentless cruelty, including the one who barged into my doctor's appointment, prying without any right. Who targets someone at their most vulnerable? I doubt they knew the hospital withheld my X-rays, but if they did, how do they live with themselves, knowing my neck was broken? Maybe it's pointless to dwell on them, but to me, they're cruel, cold, bloodthirsty, PIKES!! The apples don't fall far from the tree.

My stepfather and his sister, my biological mom, came from modest means. They had to work long and hard their whole lives to achieve their goals. He was my professor who gave me the opportunity to earn a PhD in life. Regardless of our lack of communication, his outstanding achievements and the improvement of people's lives are lessons that will never be forgotten.

I have come a long way from building houses in the bush. Working in the villages as a kid and young adult proved challenging, which is an understatement. What I faced at such a young age made me question humanity. I think trying to stay sane was tougher than enduring the brutal physical pain. As it turns out, I would find joy in other ways. With all that had happened, I found a tiny crack in heaven's enormous gates that I was able to squeeze through and gain way more than I could ever imagine. As my life started to improve quickly, a world of great joy, love, and harmony would suddenly turn into a gut punch of grief and sorrow that can never be healed.

CHAPTER 20
Beloved Son

I met my wife, Marcela, in Mexico while trying to recover. I had gone there for two reasons: I was funding my recovery, and housing and medical services were vastly cheaper in Mexico than in the States, and I figured the dry and warmer weather might improve my health. I had no idea I would find the most wonderful person in the world. I owe her my life because she gave peace in my heart.

When I first met my wife, I was frightened. It wasn't her beauty that scared me because I could tell her soul was pure, and she glowed with kindness and compassion. Not even her accomplishments in higher education and the three languages she spoke frightened me. I wasn't unnerved by her independence or determination to pay for her way and property. What frightened me was love at first sight. They say that love at first sight is more of puppy love, which is short-lived, but deep inside, I knew I would be attached to this person for the rest of my life. I just knew I would be married to her. And that's what frightened me the most.

So, I stayed away from her. I had to stay away because I had nothing to offer her. All I had was a broken body and a growing mountain of medical bills. To add to the mix, I had no job prospects, no means of making a living, no home, and no education. I had less than nothing. How would I be able to play tennis or scuba dive with her? Or keep up with her in any other way? All these issues kept running through my mind during what proved to be a long and painful recovery.

When I met Marcela, I could only walk a block or so, but I walked every day, trying to go farther and farther. The town she grew up in was small, so we often ran into each other. Eventually, we started seeing each other and were virtually inseparable.

Her family was fantastic. At the time, her father, a great man, was the town doctor and a urologist who had saved many people's lives over the years. In contrast, I brought nothing to the table. The only thing I could do was promise her that I would go back to school.

"I will need help to get an associate's degree or some sort of degree in anything," I cautioned.

That wasn't my only concern. I had countless sleepless nights worrying whether I could keep my promise because I didn't know how my life was going to work out due to all of my injuries. I didn't even know if I could get a job, but I was willing to try and not be a failure in her eyes.

As it turned out, Marcela had a highly valued degree in accounting, which meant her opportunities were unlimited. She never really liked accounting, though, so she pursued her dream of being a kindergarten teacher. I couldn't imagine anything better. She had to go back to school to obtain a master's degree, which I feared would add more pressure on me.

Thank God I had Marcela in my life. I say it again and again. Just through her compassion and enormous love for everyone she encountered, she saved me.

After our marriage, she had a lot of patience with me as I was permanently on SSI disability and carried the stress of the despicable trial that is recorded up there in Canada.

She supported me as I got my associate and bachelor's degrees at the University of Las Vegas. Eventually, I obtained a master's degree. She taught me love, compassion, happiness, and joy. Then, when things couldn't get any better, she gave me the greatest gift of all.

In our second year of marriage, Marcela became pregnant. I was excited beyond anything I could comprehend. The anticipation of seeing our child gave us such a thrill. When I first saw my son Robert's dark eyes looking up, it was as if the gates of heaven opened and allowed me to come in. My knees were wobbling, and I was smiling from ear to ear. I couldn't believe what I saw: my son, the most gorgeous person. How could I be any happier? We were beyond blessed to have a person like him in our lives.

Marcela did an interesting thing while pregnant. She only spoke Spanish to Robert. Of course, all I could do was talk in English. As he was growing up, she continued to speak only to him in Spanish while I continued speaking English. He had the best of both worlds: he spoke both English and Spanish. That would greatly benefit him, and at the very least, he could communicate with his family in Spanish whenever they visited.

That was very cool, but Robert only spoke a little, or not at all, for the first couple of years. We talked to some experts about that, and they said he was trying to figure out which language to speak, which was why it took him a little while to talk. Once he chose a language, he spoke it all the time and talked incessantly. He mostly spoke in English, which made sense since we now lived in the States. He initially spoke English to Mama, as well, so she had to push him to speak Spanish.

It was such a joyful time. We watched cartoons and did all the toddler stuff, including teaching him how to swim. I was adamant that Robert was going to learn how to swim because I knew that Alaskans have a higher rate of deaths than most other states.

Those were great days. I stayed at home, continuing to recover, and looked after Robert, eventually starting to attend school. Marcela returned to teaching Spanish and English to kindergartners. And we continued to give Robert, who was always laughing, smiling, and joyful, the happiest childhood. He was our universe, a bundle of love; we were the happiest doting parents.

We had reason to be proud. When little Robert was just over two years old, we took him to an ice cream place. He turned around, looked at the sign above the door, and read what was written on it. He wasn't talking yet, yet he had read the sign.

Wow, this child is brilliant, I thought.

Robert was a handful of positive energy and joy, and an extremely independent child. He loved to run off and do things by himself to the point that Marcela and I began to think we might need to put a leash on him. Robert didn't know it, but he helped me recover because keeping up with him was a form of exercise.

When Robert was around three, I was packing up the car in the driveway for a family vacation. I looked down and saw him sitting by the tire.

"What's wrong, Robert?"

He stared at me. "I'm tired."

"What do you mean you're tired?" I asked. "I'm just tired," he repeated.

"OK, well, you need to rest."

I was so confused. It didn't make any sense. It was mid-morning, and this was unlike him. He was a ball of energy and always on the move. I watched Robert for just a bit and then picked him up, brought him into the house, and told Marcela what was happening. We immediately called his pediatrician.

"He's OK," the doctor said. "Don't worry about anything. He probably needs a vitamin shot."

We canceled the trip and took him to the doctor. He examined our child and told us he wanted a blood test. When the results came back in, we were referred to another doctor. We didn't know what was going on. Then we got the bad news: our son had Acute Lymphoblastic Leukemia (ALL). The doctor had to explain to us that this was childhood leukemia and that Robert would need treatment for the blood disorder. The doctor could see how devastated we were. Looking us straight in the eyes, he said,

"Look, your job now is to live life. That is your mission now."

Our poor baby was subjected right away to multiple spinal injections and an assortment of pills he had to take daily. For the next several years, we had to get calendars and write down the list of pills and the exact times when he had to take them, along with the schedule for the horrific spinal taps. He did not complain once.

I went to all of his injections. I couldn't imagine what kind of pain he was in. It was awful watching that big needle tapping into his spinal cord as they injected vincristine into his spine. The irony is that dealing with my recovery gave me the time to help my son and go to all his doctor appointments. Marcela wanted to spend twenty-four hours a day with Robert, but she had to work. I felt bad for her because she suffered so much being away from him, yet she had to support the family. I could do nothing to lift that terrible burden from her.

Robert seemed more concerned about our well-being than his. He would always gaze at us with his big, warm, loving smile, even while taking his pills and getting spinal taps. He was so brave, never saying a word to us about whether he was frightened or if he was in pain. I swear, there were times when he stared at Marcela and me, and it seemed as if he was looking to comfort us, not for us to comfort him. I couldn't believe it. He was the most selfless person I've ever known—a loving spirit, a mountain of goodness, kindness, and gentleness.

Oh, how brave and strong you are. I wish I could take this cup from you, my brave little man.

When Robert was sick, we received an overwhelming amount of compassion and love from outside agencies. Great institutional charities, such as the Make-A-Wish and Candlelighters foundations, helped with some of Robert's needs. And very early on, the Make-A-Wish Foundation granted Robert his wish to go to Disney World in Florida. It just so happened that he was a big fan of *Star Wars* and got to watch the annual *Star Wars* parade. And to our great surprise, he met in private the voiceover actress who played Ahsoka, his favorite character. She gave him all kinds of *Star Wars* gifts. He had a great time in Florida. As parents, we couldn't have been happier because Disney opened their hearts and gave us special access to all the rides and attractions. Robert was delighted. Since he loved to fish at such an early age, we got him a small fishing pole so he could cast out into the nearby pond where we were staying. What do you know? He actually caught a big largemouth bass. After so many trials, it was remarkable to feel his joy.

Once Robert had completed his initial first round of spinal taps, which they call the "big blast," we were told that he had a rapid remission, which meant that they could see the white blood cell counts were heading in the right direction. Regardless, he still had years of treatment to go. The doctors wouldn't tell us much about his potential recovery if he were to survive the treatments. We didn't know what kind of outcome to expect, but we knew that when they inject people with those drugs, they kill off the good cells as well as the bad cells, which goes all the way to the brain. So, we knew he was going to have some cognitive or muscle issues.

Marcela's dad, the doctor, confirmed that there would be problems in the future and he went through some of the possibilities with us. Thank God for Marcela. She came up with the idea to put Robert into tennis immediately to help improve his hand-eye coordination, which was starting to become an issue. When he tried to climb a small three-foot ladder at my urging, I could see he had problems. He was also beginning to experience dexterity issues in his hands when using tools. Right then, I knew he would not be working in the construction industry as a laborer or anything like that. His challenges weren't that bad, but I could see where he might get hurt. And there was no way I wanted him to take a chance.

Even though Robert had been our top focus since his birth, we redoubled our efforts toward him. I wanted to treat Robert like a fragile, finely crafted piece of gold, with great respect and to deny him nothing. I didn't spoil him, but I wanted to ensure he did everything. In short, we followed the doctor's instructions. We lived.

We would take Robert to NASCAR races, which he loved because he enjoyed wearing his NASCAR hat and the remote earmuffs to hear the car races in real time. I wanted him to see the country, so we traveled with him throughout the United States, visiting thirty-four states throughout one summer. We also rented an SUV and drove to Mexico on that same trip to see his grandparents and family.

As strange as it may seem, Marcela, it turned out, came from the same Mexican town as the gentleman who wound up with my caribou. Before we were married, I had shown her the caribou in the restaurant and told her how I felt about it, what had happened, and how the caribou had come to be there. Now I wanted Robert to see it. I didn't provide any details about the hunt or why my caribou was in Mexico. I rarely discussed my time in Alaska and the villages. He just knew that it was a place I'd lived.

Our adventures took us to Texas, where we saw an enormous snake crossing the road. We went deep into the caves, learning a great deal about their formation. In Florida, we swam in the ocean, went nighttime bay fishing, and caught lots of fish, which we mounted. Then, on to New York, Mount Rushmore, and even Devil's Tower in Wyoming, which was featured in the movie *Close Encounters of the Third Kind*. We finished our trip in British Columbia so we could see his mother's friends. We also took Robert to Europe with his cousin. He got to swim in Lake Geneva, see the Colosseum in Rome, and visit the Vatican, where he was blessed.

Back in the States, I always took him on fishing trips to different parts of the country. Robert loved to catch fish and release them back into their environment, which was a family tradition taught to me by my stepfather. Every once in a while, when we wanted dinner or caught a real beauty, we'd make an exception. At the house, we still have the fish we mounted, complete with the dates and places we caught them. However, he would not allow me to hunt. I respected his wish and honored his position. I never tried to change his mind. Hunting was no longer a part of me, so I left it in the past. I did not want to distress him or challenge his point of view; it just wasn't necessary. I was fine focusing on fishing.

The adventures piled up. I even made time to go with him to New Mexico and wash our car at the car wash used in *Breaking Bad*. But we'd never visited Alaska, and Robert was on my back about that for years.

Finally, I broke down and took all of us, including his cousin, up there. We toured Anchorage and visited some fishing areas, where we caught many dolly vardens. During that fishing trip on the Kenai River, his cousin cast out, and an eagle flew down and grabbed his lure. The eagle was flying around with his cousin's lure, and he was reeling it in. It was so funny and cute, especially since the eagle got loose and flew away.

I even rented a floatplane, and we flew out to Taper Lake, the old lake cabin north of Anchorage, about thirty-five minutes by air, that my grandpa and our family had built. Unfortunately, the person we sold the cabin to had burned it down for insurance money, but they were able to see the old rock I used to swim to, as well as the river inlets and outlets I would boat to and fish.

We flew from one end of the lake to the other and around, which took some time due to its great size. They were very excited. They had never experienced anything like that before. Flying on a floatplane, taking off and landing on the water, was also a new experience. Back in Anchorage, they saw fireworks in daylight for the first time because it hardly gets dark during the summer.

Throughout the years, Marcela and I continued to do various things with Robert. As he continued to grow and live his own life, he pursued tennis and other activities. And he spent time with a special friend, another angel, he'd met in elementary school.

They couldn't explain it, but they understood each other from the very first day and became best friends. When they got together, they were like two older men in an elementary school—so serious, so happy, and so playful all the time. We couldn't be happier for Robert to have found what we considered a lifetime friendship, a soulmate, if you will.

Of course, Robert was still battling the disease at the time, taking medicines and enduring spinal taps, all without a single complaint. We transferred him to a prominent, well-known hospital on the West Coast to finish up his treatment and told this organization not to tell Robert about his disease. We knew it was getting close to the time to tell him what was going on with his body, but we still held that close to our chests. We didn't want to take Robert's childhood away from him by disclosing his disease.

"He has a right to know about his body," the doctor and the nurse insisted.

"We know, but we are going to set up a psychologist and have a group meeting to strategize about how to reveal this to him," we said. We made ourselves crystal clear to the doctor and staff.

Some time passed. One day, while he was getting treatment and I was sitting in the waiting room, I was called in. I saw the nurse staring at me strangely. I got scared.

"What has happened?" I asked.

"I told Robert what he had," she said in a weird tone.

"What are you talking about?" I exclaimed.

"Yeah, well, he had the right to know that he has leukemia."

"You weren't supposed to tell him anything. We were going to do that."

"He had a right to know."

The doctor came in right then and, with a solid, authoritarian look, echoed the nurse's statement.

"You had no right to tell him," I snapped back.

I was horrified. I could not believe that this organization had told my child about his disease without our permission.

I got Robert and took him home. I had to break the news to Marcela, and we were both shaken up. Later that night, we spoke with Robert about what he had and why we hadn't told him sooner. He wasn't the same after that. There was something different in his eyes, and the way he looked at us was very different. Sometimes, he would tell us everything was OK, but we knew something was wrong.

Later on, as he grew older, the knowledge began to hurt him. Even though he completed his treatments, he was frightened that the leukemia would return. Poor Robert was traumatized. I'm still very angry at that nurse and the doctor for what they did. It was wrong. Robert had the right to know, yeah! But he also had the right to hear the news from us, his parents. Fortunately, the breach of confidence did not hurt us as a family. We all remained close.

We had been planning a family trip. I asked Robert where he wanted to go. It was a choice between Australia and New Zealand. We decided to go to New Zealand. When we were about to buy the tickets, Marcela, who had gotten injured at work, said she couldn't travel because she'd gotten worse and could hardly move.

"I want you to go," she said.

"Wow, you're going to let Robert and me head to New Zealand by ourselves?" I asked.

"Yeah," she said. "No problem. I want you to have fun."

"OK, let's go," I told Robert. And I got to take my son to New Zealand.

It was summer in the U.S. and winter in New Zealand, so we packed for cold weather. We went to many towns, rented cars, did all kinds of things, and went fishing in a famous place, which we didn't know was that famous then. The lake was enormous and loaded with large trophy trout. I hired a fly-fishing guide, who was very kind. Robert and I had to meet the guide early in the morning. He wanted us at the boat launch at 5:30 a.m.

As we ate breakfast, I received a text from the States saying that a work colleague and a dear friend of ours had passed away that afternoon, U.S. time. Robert had been very attached to him. We regularly visited him at his house or on the bay, and he taught Robert the basics of sailing. I told Robert that we were going to catch fish for him. It was dark and cold when we left the house and drove to the boat launch. As we arrived, ice was everywhere, so we had to be careful not to slip or fall into the water. The temperature was -2.78 degrees Celsius.

We had been in the area for a few days and endured an extensive rainstorm that had caused roads to flood. Once we left the shores, I noticed all the logs the storm brought in, so I wasn't sure if we would catch anything. As I cast out, I immediately got a bite on the line. I handed the rod to Robert, and he reeled it in. It was a gorgeous, large trout like the ones we'd caught in Alaska. That was our trout together, the one for our friend. I am sure he was smiling down on us that day.

One night, we visited what turned out to be a renowned restaurant and show. The entrance was pitch black, and then we heard chanting from a distance. As the chanting grew louder and louder, we could see little flames of light approaching us. Looking down, we could see water. Within moments, a canoe arrived, paddled by the local Natives and took us to the dining area for dinner. That was part of the show, and wow, we were both mesmerized.

We then participated in the show with the rest of the audience by clapping and singing along with the Natives. Just before we ate, the host went around to each table and asked each individual to identify the language they spoke. Many guests were from all over the world, and regardless of their language, the host would talk to them in their Native tongue. It reminded me of the time when I was about fifteen and went on safari in

South Africa, where I met a man who could speak seven languages. When the host approached our table, Robert stated that he spoke Spanish, so the host talked to Robert in Spanish for quite a while. Oh, how I wish Marcela had been there.

That memorable show gave Robert and me an insight into the Māori culture, which he greatly respected. He also saw the geologic side of New Zealand and watched with great intensity the bubbling mud pools and shooting geysers that were everywhere we turned. Robert found a place where we could swim in natural hot springs. Leave it to him to discover great places to explore.

We didn't even know they filmed *The Lord of the Rings* or *The Hobbit* in New Zealand, but our travels led us to Wellington. We had gone to a hotel and restaurant for lunch, and overheard two guys at the bar talking about the movie studio for *The Hobbit*. We rudely eavesdropped on their conversation. We felt terrible doing so, but it was worth it because, as it turned out, the studio was just down the street. We got a ride over there to tour their special effects buildings.

Oh, it was so much fun to see the movie set models and the handmade armor the actors wore. We saw the arrows and axes used in battles, as well as the small and giant creatures they created, including Gollum, the little green creature who loved the ring he called "Precious." During the tour of the studio, we learned a great deal about the talent and effort that go into creating special effects. We asked where they filmed the outdoors for the movie and where the little hobbits' sets were. Once we learned where to go, we took a long drive to get to our destination and then joined a group for the guided tour, the only way we could visit the hobbits' home.

"Who's read *The Lord of the Rings*?" the tour guide asked once we were all on the bus. Robert raised his hand. When we got off the bus, the tour guide again asked who had read *The Lord of the Rings*, and Robert raised his hand again. Both times, he had been the only person to do so.

From early on, Marcela read to Robert, and thank God for her because she got Robert interested in reading. From a young age, he read constantly. Still, I was surprised that he had read *The Lord of the Rings* because it's a thick book I was never going to read.

The tour guide kept quizzing Robert about the book, which made him laugh. This young man had read the book. Many people say they've read the book, but they haven't. They see the movie. And like Robert always said, the movie differs from the book.

We were fortunate that he got to see all the Hobbit sets, including the location of the tiny home where Sam, a character in the movie, lived. We got to drink fake beer in the tavern setting and we even got to see the famous tree. However, Robert took off at some point, and I had to look for him. That streak of independence he had exhibited as a toddler was still going strong. After a long search, I finally found him. As I approached him, he was talking to a gentleman with a painting kit. He told me that the gentleman had worked on *Star Wars*.

Wow, how cool, I thought.

We asked him questions, but he refused to tell us anything about the *Star Wars* movie, saying he had signed a non-disclosure contract. The only thing he would say is that it was really neat.

We spent over two weeks in New Zealand and had the best father-son time. Robert got to see and do all kinds of stuff in New Zealand. How blessed I was to enjoy his company. God, we had so much fun. At the same time, we were disappointed that Marcela couldn't come with us because having her with us would have made the trip more joyful and complete. We decided to take her back there.

Robert loved his mom so much. She was the boss. Nothing could make me happier than knowing those two were having fun, so I was thrilled when she took Robert to Mexico by herself to visit the family. They all loved Robert, and they would share stories of their adventures. Mother and son visited Guadalajara, Guanajuato, Michoacan, and Mexico

City, where he took pictures of churches, cathedrals, and plazas, and spoke to indigenous people and tasted their unique food. He discussed the history he had learned there. Robert had loved history since childhood and constantly read historical books. Whenever we visited a historical site or a new town, he would provide a rundown of the area. Everyone in the family always said Robert was like a walking encyclopedia. He was brilliant, our go-to guy for information.

He and his mother went to an air balloon show, then ran back to stand on their relatives' roof and wave goodbye to the passengers as they passed over their heads. They told me the balloons were so close to them that it was as if they could reach out and touch them.

Then Robert climbed up the Pyramids of the Sun and Moon at Teotihuacan. Marcela and Robert walked alongside the aqueduct in Michoacan. They took the funicular to see the El Pipila statue, walked through the extremely steep and narrow streets, and joined a nighttime procession led by the Estudiantina, a group of musicians and dancers.

How cool is that?

Robert loved that trip with his mom and meeting the rest of his family. Their adventures topped New Zealand by miles because he got to be with his mom, as both were immersed in her culture.

Despite how close the three of us were, Robert could still surprise us. One night, we all went to a stand-up show for locals as an extra credit assignment for his advanced English class. The task was to listen to singers, comedians, and speechmakers, write something on the fly during the performances, and then present it on stage. From the back, my wife and I saw Robert writing down words on a napkin. He just kept writing and writing. By that point, all the other participants were now on the stage. Then we saw him tap the teacher on the shoulder and say, "I have something."

The next thing we knew, Robert was on stage reading what he had just written. It was a gorgeous, beautiful, and unbelievable poem and the audience responded with thunderous applause. We were so proud of him.

My head was spinning. I had no idea Robert could write poetry. Not a clue. He never said anything to us. He just did it.

For a long time, Robert had struggled to formulate a thesis when writing. This was his major stumbling block in English, but once he had a thesis, he was on his way to writing anything. Words just flew out of him. Sometime before graduating, we noticed that he was now fully capable of quickly analyzing written material and developing a thesis. He was so sharp, had learned so much in the advanced English classes, and had grown so fast.

"I had great teachers, and they pushed me," he told me repeatedly.

To my great relief, Robert was not dyslexic. Even when he was in elementary school, I could always ask him how to spell a word. He would be on the run up or down the stairs, and he would shout out the spelling of a word, and then smile and laugh. I always got a kick out of that.

Robert always wanted to learn and took chances by joining school clubs, such as the robotics team. He loved spending time with his new friends, working on the robots, and attending worldwide robotics competitions with his classmates.

Despite our initial trepidation about how his treatment would affect him, Robert possessed extraordinary athletic abilities, taking first place in many track races, and would eventually run in 5Ks and even a marathon. As a senior, he also took golf lessons and was a member of the high school tennis team. For the first time, their school was on a winning streak in the region. He played doubles and won everything. While competing, he would study his opponents. Once he figured them out, he used their weaknesses against them. Even so, he was so compassionate that he would sometimes lose tennis matches so his opponent would be happy with a victory.

Just before their final games and graduation, without warning, COVID-19 hit, and the schools in the U.S. shut down, bringing the games to a halt. They were robbed not only of the championship victory but of everything that a young person is entitled to. Prom, along with all the other things seniors do before graduating from high school, was canceled. I felt so bad for Robert, his friends, and all the children who were so negatively affected by the COVID lockdowns.

At the time, students had to continue their education remotely to earn their diplomas. This was not an easy time, and there was no unified clarification from our government because they were still trying to figure out what the hell was going on. Having to isolate themselves and not knowing exactly how the disease spread made for a challenging time.

After not seeing his classmates and friends for some time during the lock-down, the high school decided to have an outdoor graduation. The school used the football field to line the students up according to social distancing guidelines, and administrators called students up to the platform one by one to hand them their diplomas. It was a sunny and exceptionally windy day. The wind was blowing so hard that Robert's mortarboard graduation hat blew off, and he had to chase it down the field to retrieve it. In the end, Robert received his high school diploma and got his hat back. It was bittersweet for him to see his friends from a distance. There was no handshaking or hugging to congratulate each other.

Shortly after that, Robert also got his due in tennis, winning a doubles tournament out of state. He was so excited about the trophy he received, a glass containing twenty dollars. It proved to him that he was a champion. I teased him that now that he had won twenty dollars, he was no longer an amateur but a pro. He just smiled.

Robert enrolled in a community college, which he attended online for two years during the lockdowns. He didn't know what degree to pick.

After a lengthy discussion with his counselor, he decided to pursue a degree in English. While in high school, he had tested into a higher Advanced Placement (AP) college course in Spanish, and now he was getting a college degree in English.

What is better? I thought. *He'll be a well-rounded person.*

The school was challenging and isolating for him because he was a single child stuck with two parents who were aging before his eyes. He was supposed to be out having the time of his life. Going on dates, having fun with his friends. Unfortunately, his generation missed out on all that fun stuff. We felt terrible for him and the other students.

By then, Marcela wasn't the only teacher in the family. I had earned my teaching credential. Having to deal with students under similar circumstances, we felt as bad for them as we did for our son and his friends.

Robert took extra courses during the summer break and graduated in the winter before his twenty-first birthday. In the meantime, he volunteered extensively at an observatory, giving tours of the telescopes in both English and Spanish, and explaining the stars in the night sky. Next to the observatory was a nature center, where he volunteered to help care for the animals. He loved to help animals so much that he would spend extra time assisting the little frogs to cross the road so that they wouldn't get run over. He would catch them, walk them across the road, and then release them.

Animals seemed to love him as much as he loved them. At horse camp, they had called him "Hollywood" because he smiled and wore sunglasses all the time. They assigned him to an older, stubborn horse named Jack. Robert was the only person Jack would respond to. At the same time, Robert was doing volunteer work, he also applied to six schools. To my surprise, he got accepted to all six, three University of California and three state colleges.

Right after Robert's graduation, he went to Mexico alone and stayed with his family, whom he hadn't seen for some years due to COVID. He turned twenty-one in Mexico, and his relatives and friends took him to his first bar to celebrate his birthday. He got to see his childhood friends from when he attended school as a young child in Mexico, and they all remembered him. His cousin, who had joined our family on the Alaska trip, took courses at the university, so he took Robert to his classes on campus. He met with many of his cousins' professors, who were kind enough to discuss a possible future and courses he might want to take. Robert was also lucky to spend time with his grandmother, whom he adored, and the rest of his family.

Tragically, Robert passed away in an automobile accident just after he had decided which university he was going to attend. He was so excited to be entering that college the following semester. He was still determining what he wanted to do with his life, but he was leaning toward a career in healthcare, like his grandfather. So, he had decided to pursue a degree in Spanish at the university. That made us so proud because he could have used that degree to help even more people, which was his ultimate goal.

My beautiful son, I'm so grateful to have known a person of your quality, compassion, and kindness toward other people. It was an honor to be with you.

I didn't teach Robert that much; he's the one who taught me. Every parent probably feels the same about their child. To me, Robert was angelic—a saint, a glorious person—and I pray for him every day. I witnessed the beauty of his birth, and as I looked into his beautiful eyes, which they say are windows to the soul, I could see pure, unabashed, and unconditional love beaming from his eyes. He went through so much as a young child. I watched him muster up great courage at the age of three as he battled the cruelty of leukemia with bravery and dignity. His surviving childhood leukemia was a miracle in itself, and every day he was with us was another day of being in heaven on earth.

While I am grateful to have been on many trails, no matter how challenging, demanding, or pleasurable they were, none were as joyful and memorable as the one I traveled with my wonderful, loving wife and my gorgeous, glorious son. Among the many lessons they taught me, the most profound was the meaning of compassion, love, happiness, and joy.

Robert led the way as we followed him on his twenty-one-year trail.

Throughout my life, I have met many brave and strong people from all over the world, but never have I met anyone as courageous as Robert, for he was the bravest man I have ever known. And even more astonishing to me, the braver he was, the saintlier he became. He even sympathized with the devil.

"I feel sorry for him," he said.

I mean, the devil? Who does that? I'm not saying he liked the devil; instead, it shows his unlimited and boundless love and compassion for all of God's creations. He directed his compassion toward people and animals, and his desire to help them became an increasing obsession. His courage was infectious, and that courage transferred to his friends and to those he was helping. He would listen to others, making them his top priority. He aimed to give of himself and help those who could not help themselves. Many times, he would help others without telling us or anyone else.

Robert remained humble and quiet, never sharing his childhood medical struggles, travels, or achievements with friends or strangers. I look at all his first-place trophies and medals, including one from a baby contest in Las Vegas, among many others. Yet he never mentioned them. I say, job well done. He never wanted to make himself the center of attention, always choosing instead to show others he genuinely cared.

At Robert's celebration of life, we shared what he had accomplished in his short time here. His friends were shocked. Many of them wished they had known he had survived leukemia, saying they would have been there to help him through that trauma.

Your mom and I will never forget your trail of love and compassion. You brought mountains of joy and were loved by all who touched you. You were the best of all of us, and it is time for you to have peace and explore the grand universe. One day, we will find you, squeeze you with the tightest hug, and follow behind as you lead us on that trail of love.

That's my Trail, my Trail of Thoughts.

AUTHOR'S NOTE

This book is dedicated to my son, Robert. He wanted me to tell my story and get it published, so I decided to work hard to get it out there to the public. I hope I have done him justice.

To honor Robert's memory, some of this book's proceeds are to go to the Make-A-Wish and Candlelighters foundations. I can tell you from firsthand experience they make a difference in the children's and family's lives, fulfilling promises and giving them the ultimate gift of love from each person who contributes their time and/or donations.

All children with medical or other problems should be blessed by those who are good-natured and compassionate toward human beings. Even if you don't purchase this book, my wife and I ask that you consider donating even a small amount to either one or both of those foundations or any other children's charities of your choice (make sure they are reputable), or make a small gesture of kindness to someone. Something as simple as a hello or a smile can help turn someone in great despair toward hope, raising their spirits for a better tomorrow. I think everyone can spare a moment of their time.

I don't know if I'm religious or spiritual. What I can tell you is that I am a person with no answers as to why. Why is it the most painful and cruelest of questions for any parent to ask? As someone who believes in science, I seek proof. The vastness of the universe is beyond a human being's capacity to comprehend, and because of that, there may be something out there greater than us. What that is, I don't know, but I hope it is love for us all. As I have always told Robert, it took the universe over thirteen billion years to create you, which is why you are so special, just like all living beings are special. So, enjoy your time in this beautiful world.

Robert believed in God and felt compelled to help his fellow human beings, no matter the cost. That was just Robert. He always looked to the skies and believed in science and the universe. He kept telling me over and over, "We just change to a different form of energy when we pass on." He was a deep thinker and a brilliant human being. His friends constantly tell me how special Robert was and how he made people feel special. So, I say to you, Robert, you were LOVE and loved by all. Your compassion and love for your fellow human beings and desire to give all that you had to help others was extraordinarily selfless and will never be forgotten.

Peace Be with You, my Beloved Saint.

GOD BLESS YOU,
OUR SWEET PRINCE

2002–2023

Yellowstone Lake

Swimming with Dolphins, Six Flags, CA

Robert, Mom, Abuelo and Abuela Mexico

Robert and Mom
Rome Colosseum

Robert and I Lake Geneva, Switzerland

Robert with Mom, Dad and Cousin
Lake Geneva, Switzerland

New Zealand

Austin Powers Car Rental

Robert at the Hobbit Houses Movie Set
New Zealand

Robert and Gollum Wētā Productions
New Zealand

Robert and Bruno Grand Canyon

Robert with Cousin Heading to Cabin Lake, AK

Robert and Mom Enjoying The View of Trapper Lake Cabin, AK

Robert High School Tennis

Robert and Mom JAX SNAX Restaurant in Mexico

Robert's Fishing Trips
New Zealand, Alaska, and Oregon

Robert Standing Under My Caribou at Hotel Armida, Mexico
(Chapter 14: Bear No Hide)

Robert Proudly Standing In Front of My Stepfather's Elderberry Park Condos, Anchorage, AK Built 1978-79

Pencil Portrait of Robert by His Mom

Robert Painting by Abuela

NOTES

1 Page 18 **"National Geographic took notice..."** Wilbur E. Garrett, ed., "Hunters of the Lost Spirit," *National Geographic* 163, no. 2 (1983). https://nationalgeographicbackissues.com/product/national-geographic-february-1983/

2 Page 20 **"According to Alaska Fish and Game ..."** "Northern Pike," Alaska Department of Fish and Game, accessed November 30, 2024, https://www.adfg.alaska.gov/index.cfm?adfg=northernpike.main

3 Page 31 **"Readers interested in learning more ..."** David Lomax, "SJCC Construction Tech VDC," Lecture, Stanford Center for Integrated Facility Engineering, May 16, 2019. https://docs.google.com/presentation/d/17oM8BuuAIZFuelsR_lthXijPoP 4OvWqWr_tQaSAPkUo/edit#slide=id.g5aa4a38de5_2_128

4 Page 71 **"According to the Occupational Safety and Health Administration ..."** "OSHA Excavation Compliance," National Environmental Trainers, accessed December 14, 2024, https://www.natlenvtrainers.com/blog/article/osha-excavation-compliance#:~:text=Did%20you%20know%20the%20fatality,associated%20with%20trenching% 20and%20excavation

5 Page 185 **"Years later at college ..."** "About the Stanford Prison Experiment," Stanford University Libraries, accessed November 30, 2024, https://exhibits.stanford.edu/spe

Helio Courier

185 Float Plane

Short SC.7 Skyvan

C-119

Aviation Traders ATL-98 Carvair

UH-34D Seahorse Helicopter

www.ingramcontent.com/pod-product-compliance
Lightning Source LLC
Chambersburg PA
CBHW060415130626
46555CB00005B/2075